The Culture Watch

Robert Brustein

THE
CULTURE
WATCH

Essays on Theatre and Society,
1969-1974

 ALFRED A. KNOPF, NEW YORK, 1975

Library of Congress Cataloging in Publication Data
Brustein, Robert Sanford, (Date) The culture watch.
1. Theater—United States—Addresses, essays,
lectures. 2. Theater—England—Addresses, essays,
lectures. I. Title.
PN2266.B72   792'09   75–8227
ISBN 0–394–49814–3

For my teacher Lionel Trilling

Contents

Introduction:
The Culture Watch

I've been watching American culture for most of my life, and professionally for about twenty years—initially as a theatre critic for the *New Republic,* more recently as a regular contributor to the Arts and Leisure section of the *New York Times* (occasionally to its Magazine), and in 1972–73, during a year off from my duties at Yale, as a theatre critic in London for the *Observer.* I've watched it largely through the prism of the theatre—not only a cultural medium but, to my mind, a fundamental metaphor of American life—and even during my year away, when I reviewed the English stage, I was always throwing furtive glances over my shoulder at my native land. This book is a collection of those glances, a record of impressions gleaned from my particular vantage point over the past five years.

As cultural history, these years have been fascinating, even though the level of artistic achievement, especially in theatre, has not been spectacularly high. This looks like a paradox, but only if you assume, as I do not, that culture and art are identical. To me, the word "culture" suggests not just the theatre, music, art, dance, and literature of a society, but also the *haunted air* (as Lionel Trilling calls that intangible atmosphere) that surrounds a society's art and envelops its civilization. And since the qualities of American culture are endlessly interesting, if only because they are endlessly idiosyncratic, it has been possible for a culture watcher like me to get by during dry periods for the arts by reflecting on some of the crazy atmospheric conditions preventing growth—a consolation I have permitted myself to the point of habituation.

Admittedly, the dominant feelings exposed in this book are not pleasure and amusement but rather melancholy, even anguish and alarm. The very image of a culture watch suggests an attitude of vigilance rather than relaxation or detachment, and reading over the pieces I wrote between 1969 and 1974, I note that my language is often full of foreboding. Apocalyptic phrases flash through the prose, generally illuminating pretty much the same warning—namely, that the minority culture of art and experiment is in serious danger of being overwhelmed by the majority culture of profit and entertainment. How tiresome to keep hearing this highbrow version of a serial melodrama with its overtones of rape, seduction, and extinction of the forces of light by the forces of darkness, especially when contemporary intellectual discourse has generally agreed to treat these categories as old-fashioned. I know, in volunteering to defend Imperiled Art, that I often sound exclusive and, worse, self-righteous in my criticism of those I find responsible. I'm not happy about this, since these are hardly qualities I admire, and I'm willing to concede that I'm sometimes guilty of the failings that I detect in others. Still, what can I do except try to improve my character? I obviously can't forbear trying to improve the character of others. Somehow I've gotten it in my head that the destiny of this nation is going to be decided on a moral battlefield, which means that its future depends to some extent on how you and I behave. If we can't manage to preserve the terribly fragile and vulnerable enclave of high culture from the incursions of careerists and profiteers, then this may be a sign that this country has had it as a pluralistic society. Naturally, I speak from the standpoint of special prejudices. Although I believe that certain forms of popular culture can inform and vitalize what used to be called high art, I am by nature an incorrigible, incurable highbrow, one who still believes that the most lasting work is not always immediately recognizable and saleable. If the dangers I see are real, then the only alternative to ringing alarm bells is to remain prostrate before what is becoming a dangerous situation.

Dangerous . . . but hardly new, for the status of minority art in America has always been precarious at best. Perhaps in compensation for our unequal income structure, the country's cultural posture has traditionally been egalitarian—which is to say that difficult works, while never proscribed, have usually been treated with suspicion by the general populace (the fact that popular culture has always been enormously profitable provided cultural egalitarianism with a strong economic justification from the very beginning). With the appearance in the twentieth century of such European offshoots as the little magazine, the experimental novel, and the laboratory theatre, minority art took on the appearance of something foreign and elitist, when its practitioners were not being called renegades from democracy or threats to capitalist society.

Still, before the middle of this century, America did manage to support a pluralistic culture in spite of traditional tensions. Minority and majority art cohabited together in a state of mutual indifference: Broadway no more noticed the experimental theatre than the Big Band was conscious of the Budapest Quartet. After the "culture boom" of the fifties, however, and the emergence of what was later to be called the "arts market," minority expression itself quickly became identified as a potential source of profit and fashion (providing it could be properly assimilated into the prevailing commercial structure) and the serious artist was now solicited to adapt his work to the requirements of entrepreneurs and consumers. Just as the mass media were beginning to display the political dissenter on talk shows, thereby converting his radicalism into a form of entertainment, so the advertising agency was discovering the avant-garde painter and Broadway was encountering the experimental playwright and director, with the result that the old distinctions between highbrow, middlebrow, and lowbrow were increasingly obliterated.

Was this an occasion for celebrating the cultural coming of age of American democracy? I believed otherwise, because instead of raising the low, this kind of leveling process too often debased the high. Was culture really advanced when a gifted American composer-conductor like Leonard Bernstein transformed the Catholic Mass into a rock opera with Tin Pan Alley lyrics and flower-child epiphanies, or when a professor of classics like Erich Segal adapted Homer's *Odyssey* into a

Broadway musical? Perhaps I was being too alarmist in generalizing from such examples, but I worried about the capacity of artists and intellectuals to persevere with the work to which they had devoted their lives—partly because I knew from personal experience how difficult it was to resist such votary offerings as fame, power, money, love, and (most especially) public recognition. Writers used to joke, in past years, that "I'd like to sell out, but who's buying?" Now a lot of people were buying, a lot of people were selling, and the only problem, outside of negotiating the highest possible price, was manufacturing a sufficiently convincing self-justification.

Minority culture, in short, was beginning to lose its will to survive, besieged as it was by many within its own ranks. Some resented living under its obscure shadow, some were beginning to doubt its value, some were finding it "irrelevant" in the face of racial oppression and political inequality. The sixties were certainly a difficult decade in which to try to defend the integrity of this culture, and not only because it was being abandoned by so many of its former allies: the din of "revolution" had reached such a pitch that it almost drowned out all other sounds. For a while, everyone seemed too feverish to concentrate or reflect, and many, including me, were finding it difficult to listen to Mozart, to attend a classical play, to read the writings of Yeats or Joyce. Those who continued to affirm the value of such works were being told by intelligent people that print was obsolete, or that the existence of high culture was somehow contributing to the oppression of blacks and other minority groups. Once again, for at least the second time in a century, the world was informed that the whole of Shakespeare was not worth a pair of boots.

I spent most of those difficult years at Yale, having gone there in 1966 in an effort to help strengthen one aspect of the minority culture, the serious theatre. My determination, based on the admittedly bizarre premise that the arts and humanities were best advanced within the university structure, was to provide the idea of an experimental art theatre with an institutional foundation—part training conservatory, where young people could pursue theatrical skills and ideals, and part professional laboratory, where these skills and ideals could be put to a practical test. Such a design was fragile enough to begin with, the theatre being the most corruptible of the public arts, but for a few years it almost seemed quixotic. With an uncanny sense of timing, I had agreed to become Dean of the School of Drama just before the eruption of student unrest and participatory democracy in the American university. I originally calculated that the job would take no more than five years; nine years later, it is still not fully completed. While I hoped to see the theatre become a dwelling-place for art, I watched it first become a metaphor for revolutionary playacting, and then, when the clamor finally faded, a mirror of vanity and self-regard, an avenue to stardom and celebrity, a platform from which to catch the attention of the media.

These historical twists and turns have made the task more frustrating, but also more dramatic and challenging: in my mind, the Yale Repertory Theatre and School of Drama began to develop something of a symbolic role as an institution where the idea of serious theatre was not only embodied but also propagated and defended. Ready to do battle against the cultural levelers—whether from the right (the commercial entrepreneurs) or the left (the "revolutionaries")—my colleagues and I shared the belief that radicalism was a weapon used best not against such vulnerable targets as the university and the arts, but rather against the conditions that were helping to compromise the university and the arts—namely, the profit-seeking culture that our students were entering upon graduation. We continued to hope that young people in training could be instilled with the highest expectations for their profession, and encouraged thereby to make the greatest professional demands on themselves. If this suggested a return to the ivory tower, then so be it: it was hardly from an excess of idealism that our age was suffering, nor were selflessness and dedication among the more conspicuous characteristics of our nation.

Did we succeed in our intentions? Partly, and partly not. The last nine years have seen some extraordinarily committed theatre people coming out of Yale, and also a goodly number of careerists. For every two actors we have sent to nonprofit theatres, we have graduated another into some silly television series. And why not, you may ask, and by what right do I question the choice of fame as the world measures it? None, no right at all, except the prerogatives established by the theatre's special distress. In a less crisis-ridden age, one could afford to be considerably less demanding, but given the low estate of the American theatre, I could not help feeling my pride in a former student's rise to TV stardom mitigated by disappointment over his betrayal of his gifts. I was by nature too belligerent and impatient to imitate the saintly George Devine, who watched in silent pain while some of the most brilliant people he developed at the Royal Court abandoned their serious work for glamorous West End careers. And what weapons did I have besides the expression of disapproval and the manipulation of guilt?

At these I became such a master that I was soon able to knead a guilty spirit with the deftness of a baker forming a loaf; and every time an ex-student decided for Hollywood, or an actor dropped out of the company because he had just been offered a TV pilot, or a playwright yanked his play from our season on the basis of a Broadway offer, I would assuage my disappointment with about twenty minutes on the phone making the poor fellow squirm. What a nasty habit! And what a futile one! For whatever condition his conscience was in by the time I finished venting my moral outrage, it surely regained its former shape soon after, with nothing added but resentment. The trouble with a guilt culture like ours is that such tactics rarely produce meaningful change, and I had absolutely no desire to make people feel bad to no practical effect.

That is why I decided that my talent for producing guilt was useless and ought to be abandoned. What I discovered in its place was a capacity for producing shame, which is to say, creating a public embarrassment. For if guilt is a feeling you can endure in private without letting it affect your public actions, then shame is much more likely to have some impact on behavior. Finally, in a measure that was quite deliberate and frankly rather desperate, I decided to "go public" with my complaints. Since people tend to honor only what the society honors, it was now becoming an obligation to question our social values. Since some of our most gifted artists were being sacrificed to the majority culture, then it was necessary for the minority culture to identify this process as a source of shame.

This kind of speaking out, of course, is dangerous—not only because of the risk of embarrassment to others, but also because of the risk of humiliation to oneself. Should I fall victim, for example, to any of the traps I have described, then my own shame is multiplied tenfold, and the vice of self-righteousness is compounded by the sin of hypocrisy. This culture watch, then, is a vigil I have set on myself as well as others, and only the future will tell whether its perspective has been clouded or clear.

1
American Patrol

New Fads, Ancient Truths

The American theatre has always been peculiarly vulnerable to fashion, but it took the contemporary avant-garde to make it a victim of fads and cults: we have been subjected, in the past four or five years, to a bewildering parade of new movements, each coming on as the latest word in theatrical salvation. Stimulated by the nihilism of Pop Art, with its mischievous assault on standards and values, and cheered on by the mass media, always ravenous for new copy, the theatre has begun to announce its revolutions with all the mechanical frequency of a conductor calling stops on a commuter train, each new manifestation being hailed, before it fades from sight, as the final statement about theatre in our time. Happenings, camp theatre, the theatre of the ridiculous, radical theatre, street theatre, guerrilla theatre, new theatre, theatre of fact, nude theatre, even (I admit this blushingly, having named a book after it) third theatre—what these designate is less a record of permanent achievement than a record of historical change, amazing us more with the fickleness of taste than with much impression of artistic power.

In a way, it is refreshing to find the American theatre—after its long sleep in the forties and fifties—trying to keep abreast of the latest social, political, and sexual issues. But "relevance" can quickly get to be as empty as indifference if it is unredeemed by perception, texture, or form; it can become, in short, mere journalism. The problem with "relevance," whether on the stage or in the classroom, is its limited life. If I may paraphrase an old saw: art is long but relevance is apparently proving to be very brief.

The marriage between the avant-garde theatre and contemporary faddishness is an inevitable one in a culture where everything is bought and sold, and even words like "revolution" can quickly become as appropriate to detergent ads as to political upheaval. The one element that seems to be missing in all this conversation about the new theatre is any serious concern with the development of an artistic consciousness, either in the practitioner or the spectator—and this reminds me very much of the old theatre. What we seem to be witnessing is the upward displacement of the avant-garde into the position formerly occupied by the commercial stage, with the print media contributing the same manufactured enthusiasm previously given to Broadway. It is amusing to find the glossy weeklies and monthlies, not to mention the stately *New York Times,* embracing each new manifestation of the avant-garde with as much alacrity and as little discrimination as the *Village Voice,* building popular personalities out of Julian Beck, Tom O'Horgan, and Richard Schechner as they once did out of Joshua Logan, William Inge, and Ethel Merman. With standards being arbitrated by Madison Avenue, artistic activity becomes merely another arm of advertising, evaluated, like any other product, for its impact upon the consumer rather than for any intrinsic merit. In a situation like this, expressions like "avant-garde" and "establishment" become virtually interchangeable, and equally irrelevant to the development of a serious theatre.

In such a climate, it becomes very difficult indeed to distinguish between the artist and the publicist—even more difficult to prevent the artist's work from being vitiated by bad reproductions. The name most frequently linked with the "new theatre" is that of the Polish experimental director Jerzy Grotowski, but Grotowski seems very eager to dissociate himself from what he calls the "illegitimate children I refuse to recognize." (Stanislavski might have had a very similar response to unwanted American offspring.) In a recent interview in *Le Monde,* Grotowski complains about the impostors who claim to have mastered his technique after completing a few exercises, and who then show off the process to the public instead of completing their training—all in the name of "self-expression." "The word 'non-conformism' is bandied about," he says, "and yet there's complete conformity in the sense that every professional milieu has its five or six pet slogans (i.e., personality, freedom of the individual, sexual revolution, new society, etc). . . . Instead of getting things done, we create group hysteria and try to show that that is 'alive' and 'spontaneous.' There can be no confession without control; confession implies clarity, lucidity, and structure. Plasma and change are a confession of dilettantism."

After declaring that genuine artistic expression must be personal, not imitative, and after criticizing violent acting as a sign of immaturity, Grotowski adds: "Everyone is looking for a new theatre. Conventional theatre is a dead frog that affects great vitality, but the so-called new theatre is really the same frog resuscitated, showing superficial signs of life. And both the 'young' and the 'old' theatre try, in fact, to sell as much as possible as fast as possible." In short, the goal of much experimental theatre, like the goal of much commercial theatre, is instant success, and many of the revolutionary cries we now hear are only the most recent tokens of an old and familiar opportunism.

The situation is somewhat more complicated, and more poignant, in the case of the young whose pursuit of new theatrical forms has elements in it more desperate than careerist. I have watched some of my students embrace each new development in the theatre as if it were a signal of the Second Coming, only to drop it just as suddenly and passionately a short time later. I use the religious image consciously because it seems very clear to me that what these students are seeking in the theatre is akin to what man once sought in the Church—namely, salvation. Like most young people today, these students have embarked upon a quest for compelling alternatives to the failures of present-day society, anxious to find something that might absorb their energies and beliefs completely. The theatre is attractive precisely because it is a communal activity, and thus offers promise of the same kind of togetherness held out by T-groups, communes, encounter sessions, sensitivity explorations, and all the other current forms of quasi-tribal expression. (Some theatre groups—most notably the Daytop performers in *The Concept*—actually use these group therapy techniques before an audience.) In this kind of atmosphere, the opportunities for charlatanism are simply enormous, and a good theatre evangelist can drum up a vast following in a short period of time, provided he offers the right mixture of love and togetherness in his message.

But this, if I remember correctly, was the message of the commercial theatre in its heyday, and it makes me wonder whether the avant-garde has not managed to alter the appearance of our stage while retaining its central assumptions. Certainly the new theatre finds its identity in a similar anti-intellectualism, philistinism, and impatience with craft; and despite its distaste for the way the commercial theatre caters to the middle class, it is equally responsive to the demands of its own audiences. (In the more political forms of this theatre, writers are being pressured —as they used to be in the thirties—to confirm the hopes and aspirations of the oppressed and disadvantaged; and just as establishment critics continue to belabor Ibsen, Strindberg, Beckett, and Genet for being too difficult and arcane for middle-class audiences, so revolutionary critics reject these authors for being irrelevant to the current needs of the community.) Indeed, spectators can now satisfy their own most pressing demands by getting onstage with the actors and, instead of merely witnessing sexual exhibitionism, can strip down to their underwear and swing along with Mitch. What is being sacrificed in all this community groping is the far-reaching vision of the gifted author. Chekhov used to inveigh against the pressure to bring Gogol down to the people instead of bringing the people up to Gogol. Today we should be more worried about losing Gogol altogether beneath a pile of bodies on the stage.

The contempt for individual truth in this country—indeed, our growing disaffection from art itself—may someday be measured in parallel with the transfer of cultural power from the mature to the young, the transition from Freudian analysis and its hard biological truths to group therapy with its soft social relationships, the growing reluctance of audiences to observe rather than participate, and the substitution of open confession and public display for privacy, contemplation, and solitude. It will also be measured in parallel with our weakness for fads and cults. For all these developments are the by-products of a culture that has lost its confidence and its direction, a culture for whom the herd instinct has begun to manifest itself as a defense against loneliness and frustration.

But there is another defense against these terrors, which we owe to the Greek way of thought. It is found in the capacity to live without salvation, to accept the hard consequences of being human, to develop a tragic sense of life. What great art shows us, and particularly the theatrical art of tragedy, is how to endure with courage and strength in the face of the emptiness of life. It neither shrinks from this emptiness nor surrenders to it; it understands simply that even in the most perfect society devised by men, there will always be loss of youth, incertitude, and death. Rather than being a defense of the status quo, as some have charged, the tragic art is a notable act of rebellion against existence; rather than consoling its audience with false hopes and shallow doctrines, it offers the shared comfort of ritual union in the harmoniously created action. "Dare to be tragic men," wrote Nietzsche, "and ye shall be redeemed." Neither our avant-garde nor our commercial theatres have ever shown much interest in this kind of redemption; only O'Neill, among our dramatists, ever aspired toward it, not fully achieving it until his last plays. Until our theatre can learn to absorb the tragic sense, it will always be subject to fads, cults, and fashions; indeed, until we ourselves can learn to be tragic men, our lives will be disappointed, delusionary, confused. (1969)

The Yale Idea
An Address to Students at the School of Drama

On behalf of the faculty, the company, and the staff, I am very pleased to welcome you to the Yale School of Drama—those of you who are entering these halls for the first time, and those who have been rampaging through them for one or two years now. You are entering upon, continuing, or completing a training career during what may be the most tumultuous time in academic history—a period when learning institutions, which were always assumed to be durable if nothing else, have become extremely vulnerable to internal and external pressures, and may, in some cases, be in danger of collapsing altogether. Certainly never before, in the memory of some of us, have the universities served as such a barometer of national calamities. An invasion begins in the Far East, and as a dire result, four students are killed at Kent State University. The military conducts war research, and an innocent graduate student in physics is blown up in a building in Wisconsin. A trial begins in New Haven, and the normal academic expectations of a large institution called Yale are suspended or modified for the remainder of the term.

It is obviously becoming impossible for somebody to sneeze in the Pentagon without causing an epidemic of pneumonia in the Academy. Never before have governmental causes had such immediate educational effects. As a result, those who function within the university have grown extremely sensitive to the crises afflicting this nation, perhaps more sensitive than anybody else in America. Also as a result, the customary stereotypes no longer apply. It is not Academia but rather the White House that can now be called an ivory tower. It is not the professoriate but rather Nixon and Agnew who seem to be cut off from the pressing demands of the country, and indifferent to its urgent concerns.

For this reason, one can understand why some would want to hold the university accountable for the sins of the Nixon administration: it is sensitive, available, and there. On the other hand, to treat the university as a surrogate for the government—simply because it is more vulnerable and accessible than the government—is impractical and cowardly. For the university, despite its faults, remains, I believe, the best hope of the country, and its destruction promises only a more brutalized future.

I bring this up in order to plead for the preservation of the university's research function at a time when many are demanding that it become an instrument of social utility and political change. This means preserving its strict autonomy and independence from any ideology, even that developed out of the most humanitarian motives. Students and faculty are sensible enough to see that the university must completely sever its ties with the military-industrial complex, but they are not sufficiently consistent to demand the university's separation from all extra-academic interests, including the very pressing and necessary needs of the surrounding community. If we don't think thoughts here in the university, if we don't experiment and research, if we don't continue along what may seem useless and idiosyncratic paths, then we are all doomed to become actors—and poor actors, at that—performing roles for which we are ill-suited, and incapable of playing the parts we can do well.

This exhortation is a preface for a brief description of what we are doing at the Yale School of Drama. Like American society, the American theatre is ailing, and we at Yale are experimenting to find a cure. We've been doing this for four years now, going into a fifth. The last four years have seen a lot of trial and error, common to all experiments, and there is no guarantee that we will not commit errors in years to come. But the health, confidence, and achievement of the Yale Repertory Theatre over the past five or six months is a promising sign that we may at last have broken through to the sun.

Let me try to describe something of our history, in order to suggest our aims and how we have tried to reach them. We have been driven by a single overarching idea: to discover, during a time when the theatre seems to have lost its way, the means by which to create theatrical works of art. This idea is instrumented in two ways—through a functioning theatre and a training school—because we have been aware from the beginning that a theatre art was impossible until people were developed who could create it. George Balanchine, I believe, came to a similar realization in developing the City Center Ballet, and so he built his company not out of existing materials but out of people he personally trained. But ours is the first professional theatre company in the United States, if I am not mistaken, to develop organically out of a training program at a school.

Our beginnings were necessarily tentative and tortuous, primarily because we had to tread water a little until our first group of students went through their three-year program. The first year (1966–67)—probably the most spectacular in terms of conventional theatre successes—was based on the principle of "pickup casts," chosen from among the more gifted artists in England and America, doing the most interesting experimental projects available. This was the year of *Viet Rock, Dynamite Tonite, Endgame, Volpone,* and Robert Lowell's version of *Prometheus Bound.* The people who worked with us that year—Kenneth Haigh, Jonathan Miller, Irene Worth, Clifford Williams, Paul Sills, Ron Leibman, Linda Lavin, David Hurst, Billy Redfield, Gene Troobnick, Alvin Epstein—were available because they were on short-term loan and were always willing to do an exciting role in a single production. And it was hard to suppress the temptation to go on organizing a season on the basis of a project idea, rather than a company ideal, in the manner of commercial producers and impresarios.

But the idea of a repertory company was intimately connected with the idea on which the whole enterprise was begun. And so the next year (1967–68), we made our first attempt at ensemble, gathering together a group of actors from various places and traditions—Stacy Keach, Ron Leibman, Michael Lombard, Kenneth Haigh, Estelle Parsons, Barry Morse, Anthony Holland, Robert Jordan, and Kathleen Widdoes. That second year had its notable successes also, but we soon discovered that, for a variety of reasons, we could not force a company into existence merely by putting a group of actors together in the same location. Something more cohesive and binding was necessary, and so before the year was over, most of the actors had vanished, drawn to more commercial careers or hounded away by students competing for the same stage space.

Our third year (1968–69) was undoubtedly the low point in the history of the Yale Repertory Theatre, as well as being the most depressing period of my own life. The theme of our season that year was disruption, revolution, and violence, and, beginning with a visit by the Living Theatre, we managed to live that theme in action. Some of our productions were heckled; two were canceled partly as a result of student tumult; everybody had a different idea about what we were supposed to be doing. And it began to look as if the university, which I had once thought ideal for a theatrical renaissance, was a particularly forbidding and inhospitable place for anything having to do with the imagination.

That year was our Armageddon and, having passed through it, we finally entered upon a time of possibility (1969–70). The students who had been clamoring for three years for their own place in the sun had finally completed their apprenticeship, and were ready to give the company roots. And despite all the intensity of their previous feeling, despite their grumbling and protests, despite their questions about the directions of the training and the quality of the instruction, they nevertheless managed, upon stepping onto the repertory stage, to display that harmonious ensemble work we had been awaiting for three long years. Without even being aware of it, they had been growing together like a symbiotic organism during their period of apprenticeship; and the common air they breathed, the common goals they shared were beginning to find expression through the agency of a theatre ensemble.

But now that the Yale Repertory Theatre has taken root and begun to embody the idea on which it was founded, the training at the school has necessarily taken on a very special complexion. This training is based on the assumption that among the great failures of the American theatre, along with its lack of courage and imagination, has been its rampant amateurism —its illusion that those involved in theatrical enterprises, unlike those involved in dance, music, architecture, and painting, do not have to know anything special about their profession. We believe otherwise; and we are dedicated here to training you in the various skills of your disciplines, and to opening for you the various artistic possibilities to which these skills may be lent. We believe this can be learned through a combination of theory and practice, through classroom exercises and production experience. And we believe that after you have been sufficiently exposed to the agonies and satisfactions of a training situation—only then will you be prepared to face an audience in a professional theatre.

So the training is designed to expose you to the techniques of theatre, to each other, and to the atmosphere of professional theatre—in the expectation that these various exposures will eventually fit you for a healthy career in a satisfying kind of theatre. To be blunt about it, the School of Drama is now functioning as a conservatory for the Yale Repertory Theatre—and no longer as an isolated academic degree-granting institution—in the hope that your training and talent will eventually serve our company, or permanent companies like it. I will not emphasize the great employment advantages, in a profession where the great majority are permanently out of work, to be gained from the possibility of entering a company directly out of a school. It is our experience that many of you can't comprehend this until you graduate and directly experience the harsh reality. But it is necessary to remember the advantages implicit in the possibility of these deferred pleasures when mourning the loss of immediate gratifications. And to take advantage of the training rather than grieve over lost opportunities (as so many students do when they finally leave school).

I have tried to suggest some of the advantages of company work: the economic security of an ongoing situation, the opportunity to stretch yourself in a variety of roles rather than remain stuck in one marketable area, the rewards of a robust creative community sharing the same values and goals. But I have said nothing yet about the vision that such a theatre serves. For there is something beyond a theatre ensemble that justifies its existence—an idea of the theatre that the company both embodies and subordinates itself to. This can be best defined through the work itself, as dramatized on the stage. But if I were to describe our purpose—the idea of our theatre—it would be in terms of creating out of inherited and invented dramatic materials an art significant for our time.

We are concerned, in short, not with fashion and novelty so much as creating a contemporary poetry of the stage, developing metaphors for our time that speak to us of our current nightmares, hopes, and afflictions. Our theatre is a research theatre, a laboratory designed not to solve problems but rather to analyze them correctly—a theatre with a metaphysical life, immediate without being vulgarly "relevant," vital without being activist.

We are not interested in "good theatre" per se, or with mounting masterpieces out of misplaced academic piety— nor do we believe that the theatre must be continually invented anew without any reference to what has gone before. If we do a play, we have to believe it has the power to provoke and enlighten; and we intend to indulge our penchant for experiment, even at the risk of occasionally alienating our audience. This means our work is oriented neither towards the spectator (though hopefully it will appeal) nor towards the performer (though hopefully he will be satisfied with his roles) so much as towards an idea: to keep the theatre alive as a medium of direct experience where human beings can involve themselves in imaginative enterprises without the obstacle of a movie or a television screen.

These remain ideals rather than consistent achievements; and we hope, as I say, that the meaning of our theatre will display itself on our stage. In one sense, it is already beginning to display itself in the faces of the company. The actors have now begun to think of themselves with some pride, exuberance, and happiness—and possibly a little smugness, too—as an effective community of artists. What now shows in their faces is the validation of those difficult four years. It is the validation of the training at the school. And it will eventually validate, I believe, all your own anguish and impatience. Out of soil like that, something handsome, hardy, and strong is bound to grow. (1970)

A New Conspiracy Theory

Lenny

Add to your collection of conspiracy theories the proposition that a secret agreement exists between the Justice Department and the entertainment industry—the one committed to creating a fixed quota of judicial martyrs, and the other to selling plays about them to a comfortably indignant audience. As supporting evidence for this theory, take note of how frequently we have been scandalized, in recent seasons, by the theatricalized legal hassles of the Berrigans, the Rosenbergs, Abbie Hoffman and Jerry Rubin, and J. Robert Oppenheimer. Next year, if the conspiracy holds, we may confidently expect a rock musical on the subject of the Pentagon Papers, brought to Broadway by the lucky producer who managed to get an option on the trial of Daniel Ellsberg.

I flatter myself that this notion might have appealed to Lenny Bruce, and that he might have spun a routine around it. For it was Bruce who taught us to see all of American life as a venal extension of show business, with politics, religion, justice, even history itself, functioning as façades for commercial exploitation. To Bruce, the Church was a racket to sell luminescent crucifixes; politicians were created to order by talent agencies; and the judicial system provided the best opportunities available for showmanship. (Bruce's obsessive ambition during his own legal troubles was to do a stand-up act before the Supreme Court.) How ironic, then, that Bruce should ultimately become a martyr to his own vision—first being victimized by the same legal system he lampooned, and now by the very entertainment mill he so loathed and reviled. To discover Lenny Bruce cast as the posthumous hero of the new socko play with music at the Brooks Atkinson Theatre is to find our conspiracy theory further confirmed, since Broadway has effectively completed a process of falsification initiated by the courts.

The name of this item is *Lenny,* and I must confess I found it a pretty unsavory affair. Apparently designed as a tribute to Bruce, the play tries to combine an appreciation of his talent with episodes from his life, including his marriage, his nightclub career, his trial on charges of obscenity, and his death from an overdose of heroin. But although the work is meant to be a testimonial to Bruce's struggle for free expression, *Lenny* manages to assimilate its hero into another tradition entirely, making him acceptable to audiences who would never have liked him, and unrecognizable to those who did. Many familiar Bruce bits are represented in *Lenny,* borrowed from *The Essential Lenny Bruce* and delivered by a glossy young actor named Cliff Gorman. But something very odd—and very unhealthy—has happened to the transfer to the stage, with the result that Bruce, for the first time in my experience of his work, actually does begin to seem (what is the word?) a little . . . dirty.

The fault lies not with the actor, who does an energetic if somewhat uninflected impersonation of the comedian. (Gorman's energy somehow never reaches his eyes.) Nor can it be attributed to the playwright, since Julian Barry's text, while clumsy, at least tries to remain faithful to Bruce's spirit. The person responsible, I am afraid, is the director, Tom O'Horgan, whose irrepressible theatrical antics continue to dominate and distort all his projects. This particular evening, for example, intermittently features a parade of witch doctors, lepers, and creatures looking like Abominable Snowmen, the last dressed in burlap with strings hanging from their noses like snot, who cavort about the stage playing weird musical instruments. Then Bruce is permitted a feverish dream sequence peopled by some of the creatures of his imagination (Eichmann carrying a glass booth, Hitler on enormous stilts), who seem to have wandered in by mistake from the Bread and Puppet Theatre. The stripper whom Bruce marries remains practically naked throughout most of the play (even when Bruce brings her to meet his mother), and when they first make love, we are invited to observe their pre- and post-coital play, including an extended bit of mimed cunnilingus. Virtually all Bruce's solo routines have turned into big production numbers with large casts, while the "Religions Inc." bit now features two muscular long-haired hippies (apparently on loan from *Hair*) who play Moses and Jesus totally naked. Even Bruce is forced to participate in the obligatory O'Horgan nude sequence, when a trolley tracks out of the mouth of a stone head of Nixon (apparently responsible for Bruce's death, though he wasn't elected until two years after) revealing Bruce's naked body draped over a toilet bowl.

Now Bruce, for all his audacity and daring, was not a sexual exhibitionist, never performed a pornographic routine, and rarely felt any strong compulsion to expose his genitals to the public (though he did allow himself to be photographed once on a latrine). His comedy, as a matter of fact, can best be characterized in the same way Judge Woolsey once described Joyce's *Ulysses*—as more emetic than erotic. It is true that Bruce's language, for which he was indicted, did involve a generous use of four- and ten-letter words; but his obscenities were designed less to arouse prurient interest than to desanctify ritualized objects and to deflate hypocritical ideals. To surround Bruce with camp pyrotechnics, nude charades, Expressionistic Busby Berkeley bits, La Mama phantasmagoria, and other fruits of O'Horgan's overripe imagination, is not only to betray Bruce's lean, skeptical Jewish spirit but, worse, to identify him with a Puritan tradition (camp and pornography being inverted forms of Puritanism) that he despised.

To be sure, there is one way in which he is linked to this tradition. As the script of *Lenny* makes excessively clear (Bruce's routines are often followed by long-winded descriptions of their redeeming social value), the comedian's doomed and poignant conflict with the law over free expression ultimately helped to lay the groundwork for our present-day unprecedented cultural and artistic freedom. And it is undoubtedly true that without the example of Lenny Bruce, there would be no *Oh! Calcutta* or *Che,* no X-rated films, no *Futz* or *Tom Paine* or *Hair*—indeed, no *Lenny*. On the other hand, there are those (possibly including Bruce himself if he were still alive) who might not be so eager to count this among his highest achievements, since despite the obvious social importance of an uncensored theatre, the products of this development have thus far seemed more sensational than illuminating.

Ultimately, the greatest tribute that the creators of *Lenny* could have paid Bruce was to present him in all his freshness, uniqueness, and singularity. He was obviously one of the few performing geniuses of the postwar period. But to thank him for his pioneering work by assimilating him into our current opportunist conventions and vulgar theatrical fashions is to make gratitude indistinguishable from rancor. With *Lenny*, as with *Hair* before it, Tom O'Horgan has demonstrated an extraordinary gift for translating whatever is dangerous, inaccessible, spiky, tough, and difficult into smooth entertainments suitable for easy consumption by Broadway audiences. He has exposed, in short, the secret alliance that exists now between the American avant-garde and middlebrow taste, between pornography and Puritanism, between the illusion of radicalism and the demands of the box office. It is, finally, with Mr. O'Horgan and his associates that our conspiracy theory begins to take on weight and validity, for it is they who invariably reduce every form of legitimate art and protest into harmless foodstuffs for the jaded palates of the radical chic.   (1971)

Cultural Schizophrenia

It seems likely that if the cultural history of this era ever comes to be written, then the postwar period, and particularly the last decade, will be seen as the time of America's greatest moral collapse and intellectual confusion. So profoundly unsettling are these conditions, in fact, that even the publication of such a record becomes somewhat problematical. Now that the traditional function of history as an effort to evaluate human events objectively is under assault, and now that the culture itself has become a grab bag of careerist advancement and media opportunism, "cultural history" may soon become another disposable item—like philosophy, classic languages, pre-twentieth-century literature and drama, pure science, and all those other artifacts of the curious period preceding our present Great Age of Relevance. On the other hand, since it is customary for disintegrating societies to chronicle their own degeneration, it is not unlikely that some modern Tacitus may even now be observing our inexorable march toward ethical, spiritual, and artistic bankruptcy, preparing ample documentation of the great chasm that presently exists between our proclamations and our achievements.

As the seventeenth-century commentator Richard Burton determined that the Elizabethans suffered from a malady called melancholy, so our modern historian may conclude that we are weak from an illness called cultural schizophrenia, and offer a diagnosis without too much hope of a cure. For cultural schizophrenia is identified by the divided character of its victims—these victims being a number of artists and intellectuals, and many academics as well—which makes them desire simultaneously to be serious and respected and to be rich, famous, and popular. To be sure, these symptoms have always been present in America, but largely because of our country's long indifference to serious literature, they have rarely been allowed to blossom into full-scale sickness. For most writers in the past, therefore, the choices were simpler: either to remain single-mindedly devoted to one's calling, like T. S. Eliot and Edmund Wilson, or to separate one's creative from one's moneymaking and moviemaking activities, like William Faulkner and F. Scott Fitzgerald, or to sell out completely, like Clifford Odets, for a Hollywood pool. But something happened in the fifties—something symbolized by the marriage of Arthur Miller and Marilyn Monroe—that broke down the hitherto firm boundaries between culture and show business, and sent writers scurrying after celebrity with the clamorous encouragement of Hollywood, Broadway, television, publishing, the newspapers, and the mass magazines.

All this coincided with the coming of age, after World War II, of a large college-educated middle class, demanding products from the newly developed "arts market"—accompanied by the postwar frenzy for change stimulated by the new speed of communications. The "cultural explosion" was beginning to ignite; university education had achieved a new status after the humiliation of Sputnik; and intellectuals, and later academics, were gaining the kind of prominence formerly enjoyed only by the most famous serious novelists like Hemingway and Thomas Wolfe. The enforced isolation of America's writers had come to an end.

Soon Hollywood discovered there were big grosses to be had from movies based on serious literature, and not just *Anthony Adverse* or *Gone with the Wind*. Publishers were paying huge advances to authors for unwritten books, which were quickly recouped through book clubs and paperback rights; the literary and academic celebrities thus created were being toasted on a host of television talk shows; *Playboy* and *Nugget* started slipping in short stories and literary interviews between the pages of their cartoons and nude photographs, while *Vogue* and *Harper's Bazaar* fit poetry, stories, and reviews among their clothing, cosmetic, and jewelry ads; writers were invited to participate in symposiums on every conceivable topic, and to write for the mass magazines on every current subject; and prominent personalities began enjoying incomes of over $100,000 from lecture tours alone. We were into an age where the appetite for fame joined the hunger for money as the decisive factors in the direction of many careers, and everybody who could hold a pen was in a position to be as famous as a movie star.

Partly as a result of this development, the efforts of a previous generation to preserve the divisions between high, middle, and low culture were seriously compromised, if not entirely swamped. In the fifties, a vigorous debate had taken place between the social scientists and the little-magazine intellectuals over the relationship of the serious writer to a mass audience. At that time, the sociologists took an essentially egalitarian position, declaring culture to be of value mainly as a statistical phenomenon, and therefore analyzing forms (comic books, movies, popular lyrics, television shows) that had the widest possible appeal, while the literary intellectuals adhered to a basically highbrow position that defended the integrity of the vanguard artist in the face of pressures on him to simplify his work or conform to popular taste. It was something of a paradox, at that time, to find leftist intellectuals arguing in favor of what looked like cultural aristocracy, but the paradox was only apparent. Despite their insistence on excellence, the intellectuals maintained a consistent radicalism in their opposition to the manipulation of culture for profit, their insistence on freedom of artistic expression, and their desire to raise the level of taste rather than lower the quality of art—while the social scientists, despite their liberal democratic posture, were apologizing, however unwittingly, for Madison Avenue's engineering and debasement of popular taste.

Political radicals and highbrow intellectuals alike found a home in magazines like *Partisan Review*—magazines that enjoyed an influence well beyond their small circulations. This influence was achieved through the contributions of men and women who made up America's last great intellectual community—Philip Rahv, Dwight Macdonald, Lionel and Diana Trilling, Irving Howe, William Phillips, Mary McCarthy, Paul Goodman, Hannah Arendt, Eric Bentley are representative names—whose writing usually included attacks on the falseness of this particular novel, the sleaziness of that particular play, which had somehow attracted public attention and been inflated beyond its worth. If there was something severe and puritanical in these cultural strictures, there was also something passionate and engaged, as if years of totalitarianism had underlined the fragility of free thought and authentic art, and demonstrated the need for continual vigilance to keep them alive. Macdonald, in particular, was always ready in those days to man the barricades against middlebrow culture (or "midcult" as he called it, using a term that itself owed something to the mass media), bombarding philistines with the same lively style he used to direct against Stalinists, with the declared purpose of preserving standards in a market economy.

The emergence of a new form of political radicalism in the sixties, however, completely altered the terms of this debate, and threw the intellectual world into total confusion. For where the highbrow leftist of the fifties found himself in conflict with the middlebrow money ethic of the liberals, the new political radicals demonstrated how it was possible to be avant-garde, popular, and rich, all at the same time. In short, the same arguments advanced previously by liberal sociologists on behalf of mass culture were now being adopted by self-declared revolutionaries in support of the "counterculture," while the standards of the intelligentsia, along with the creations of difficult artists, were denounced as élitist and anti-social. (It was not long, indeed, before art and intellect themselves were to fall under suspicion as bourgeois forms of Western decadence.) Whereas the left intelligentsia were caught in a seeming contradiction between their radical politics and high cultural values, the counterculture had the advantage of ideological consistency. Representing itself simultaneously as a mass movement—using new popular forms created by and for youth—and an adversary movement—making war on all established forms and traditions—the counterculture thereby appeared to provide a bridge between political and cultural radicalism, reconciling the conflicting demands of popular taste and revolutionary resistance.

In this, it received support from the new McLuhanism, which, while declaring the obsolescence of such high forms as the novel, the poem, and the play, paid craven homage to the mass media, using a mode of analysis wholly empty of moral or aesthetic criteria. Scrutinizing culture from the viewpoint of the consumer rather than the artist, always concerned with impact rather than quality, McLuhanism thus provided the intellectual cornerstone for the exploitation of the media by the counterculture and the exploitation of the counterculture by the media, raising entrepreneurship to a new eminence, and elevating the importance of the spectator in all performance events. At the same time, a genuine concern over racial inequality, poverty, and the continuing Vietnam war was being used as a scourge against all art that did not try to change the world or alter consciousness or provide ideological instruction; and the whole construct of artistic standards was being dismissed by way of analogy with oppressors imposing their privileged laws on the oppressed. In short, totalitarian concepts of culture began to reappear under the guise of a revolutionary politics.

In the face of this onslaught—in the face of the capacity of the counterculture to manipulate the media, intimidate its critics, declare its revolutionary aims, and enrich itself all at the same time—the energies of the minority intellectuals seemed to dry up and wither away. Some grew silent, others tried to continue the debate but were shouted down, still others changed sides and joined the counterculture, consoled by the thought that they were remaining in the young radical swim. *Partisan Review,* once the champion of Kafka, Joyce, and Eliot—indeed the very locus of American intellectual values—was publishing articles on the glories of Camp and Underground films, along with encomiums by its own editors on the artistic power of the Beatles.

In a parallel development, university teachers, intimidated by cries of relevance, were beginning to surrender their commitments to literature, philosophy, history, and psychiatry, and, under the rubric of curricular reform, were offering courses in magic, astrology, rock music, Yoga, Zen, and meditation. Charles Reich, a law professor, advised us to seek salvation in bell-bottom trousers and love beads. Leslie Fiedler, a literary critic, was devoting his attention to Frank Zappa and the Mothers of Invention. Hair grew longer; alcohol gave way to pot and acid and amphetamines; costumes grew more garish and outlandish. Instructors began vying with each other for the largest enrollments, and even wider exposure through television. And cultural schizophrenia, infecting young and old alike, began to spread like a plague throughout the land. . . .

In the kingdom of cultural schizophrenia, Norman Mailer is unquestionably the emperor—the most celebrated figure in the pantheon, he completes the court and sets its style. A man who has made his writing virtually inseparable from his personal ambitions—wholly identified as the self-made hero of his self-created drama—Mailer is now almost completely consumed by his theatrical personality, which he displays at will on public platforms, in electoral campaigns, in novels and journalism, on television, and finally (and inevitably) on celluloid, where he appears as the star of his own films. Mailer may singlehandedly constitute one of the greatest public-relations firms in America, since he is able to generate his own publicity, write about it, and sell it simultaneously. Mailer is nothing if not interesting; he has the instinct of a brilliant improvisational entertainer. What Mailer possesses in superabundance is style, both as a writer and as a personality, and he has managed to use this style like a spinning disc to hypnotize virtually the entire world—including many perceptive intellectuals—into thinking not only that he is an emperor but that he is splendidly garbed.

One of Mailer's more ingratiating qualities is his self-honesty; openly declaring his Napoleonic ambitions, he disarms his critics and defuses their judgments. And Mailer has not been reticent about his extreme competitiveness, his desire for influence, his lust for fame. In his first book of proclamations, appropriately called *Advertisements for Myself,* he announced that he had been running for President all his life; as if to show that he was not speaking metaphorically, he has since campaigned for Mayor of New York City. Precariously balanced between clown and prophet, continually trying to join celebrity with seriousness, Mailer has proceeded remorselessly along his extraordinary career, cheered on from the sidelines by a growing army of intellectuals, camp followers, magazine editors, and urban sophisticates who hope to find in Mailer's cultural schizophrenia the justification for their own.

Given these conditions, Mailer's determination to make movies with himself as director, producer, writer, and star was an inevitable development. In a recent issue of *New American Review,* Mailer has even offered to function as his own critic and theoretician as well, in a brilliant coup of personal press-agentry. His article, entitled "A Course in Film-Making," is a quasi-academic discourse on the making of films, conceived by a man who has thus far made only two home movies, both of them pretty wretched. As for the theory, which Mailer calls "a Leviathan of a thesis," it is a compound of rather pompous abstractions—most of them either banal or wrong or both—about the distinctions to be made between theatre and film, film and the novel, movie acting and stage acting, and so on.

But the thesis is always subordinate to, and in the service of, Mailer's self-promotion. Identifying himself in this essay as "the director," Mailer proceeds to describe his film as a perfect example of his new theory, comparing its photographic effects to those of *Citizen Kane*, praising the actors (including himself) for being "more real . . . more vivid than in other films," and eulogizing his theory, his movie, and himself in what amounts to a perfect orgy of autointoxication:

He had a conception of film which was more or less his own, and he did not feel the desire to argue about it, or install himself modestly in a scholar's catalogue of predecessors and contemporaries; it seemed to him naturally and without great heat that *Maidstone* was a film made more by the method by which it had been made than any film he knew. . . . But his film was his own, and he knew it, and he supposed he could write about it well enough to point out from time to time what was special and mysterious in the work. . . .

But ultimately the quality of the movie is less important to him than its capacity to function as an event in the drama of his career. (He had already planned, if he decided the movie was a disaster—admittedly a pretty unlikely conclusion—to turn it into a documentary about the making of a bad movie.) Even the plot of the film signifies its purpose in Mailer's fantasy of himself, since it takes place after the assassination of an American President, at which time "this film director [played by Mailer] would be one of fifty men whom America in her bewilderment and profound demoralization might be contemplating as a possible President. . . ." Thus we can see the escalating spiral of ambition inspired by Mailer's cultural schizophrenia where he becomes a director of pornographic films, like the director in *Maidstone,* in order to become famous enough to be considered eventually for the presidency of the United States.

At this point, cultural schizophrenia seems to fade into political paranoia—though as this wild country has repeatedly demonstrated, delusions of grandeur may soon lose their delusory quality if held persistently enough by determined people. We have seen how Mailer has journeyed over the years from a competent novelist to a highly praised journalist, to a charismatic culture hero, and now to a movie star-director, always reaching for that mass acclaim first generated by Hollywood. Now it seems that the pinnacle of media fame may be only a stepping stone to political ambition. And cultural schizophrenia—in a nation that makes governors and senators out of its movie stars—can be an impulse not only toward riches, fame, and popularity but toward the will to power as well.

What is being lost from the cultural schizophrenics, however, is the hope of a serious body of thought or an important body of art. America is a land notorious for waste, but the waste of sheer creative energy exhausted in the making of careers will not be the least of the sins for which we will answer to history. American writers are finally beginning to gain the "community" they have been seeking with a larger audience; but this community merely mirrors the failures of the country through a coarse reflecting prism. Certainly a sufficient number of our best writers have successfully resisted the lures of the media and continued to perform important work; but it is nevertheless true that America's cultural life over the past decade has been characterized by a rapid degeneration in courage, honesty, vision, and quality. We have been witnessing a modern *trahison des clercs,* signified by the surrender of men and women with great potential to whatever is pernicious in American society. And this is ultimately the tragic side of cultural schizophrenia: that it wears down resistance and stains the soul, that it barters away not only the self but the very possibilities of life and art.   (1971)

On the New Cultural Conservatism

In its Summer 1972 issue, the editors of *Partisan Review* asked a number of writers to address themselves to the following proposition:

There is, we think, a growing conservatism in discussions of what's happening in the arts, and particularly in writing and thinking. A querulous tone is becoming increasingly apparent in the assessments of the tendencies and experiments of the past decade. One can see, too, a noticeable reluctance to receive new works, new writers, new forms, with anything like the generosity that might have been expected even five years ago. There is a marked suspicion of any deviation from the accepted notions of seriousness, as there is of any departure from the orthodox version of the mainstream.

Of course, a good deal of contemporary art does exploit the idea of the new, and does feed on the cult of immediacy. But the new cultural conservatism both exaggerates and revels in the failings of dissident and younger talents, and blurs the distinction between original work and radical postures; it inflates established figures, and celebrates old values, old works, old institutions as though they can never be changed or added to or replaced. Essentially it represents a hostility to anything exploratory, problematic, and disquieting, and it in fact often goes along with a rejection of the whole modernist impulse in art.

Conservatism does not always take the same form in culture as in politics, nor is the relation usually predictable. As we know, many "advanced" writers, like Dostoevski and Eliot, held conservative views. But there does seem today to be some correspondence between the political and cultural drifts to the right. There are contradictions, but usually the people and the publications that feel threatened by radical politics also feel at home with more familiar art, and with the culture of the past, particularly with that part of it which serves to bolster received values and ideals and to favor certain types of traditional themes and conventional structures.

We asked a number of people if they agreed with our sense of this situation. Did they think the stand we have described is a legitimate act of criticism? Or is it simply a nervous response, an attempt to reverse things by dismissing them?—a reaction of the kind that new culture turns have always aroused. By whom and where is the new conservatism expressed? What does it mean for the immediate future of new writing, painting, theatre, music?

The comment that follows was my attempt to respond to these questions.

I am interested in the argument you advance but I am not certain you formulate it correctly. Your statement strikes me as rather defensive—an uneasy probe into the criticism being directed toward certain intellectual journals (including your own) that may have grown too infatuated with the fashionable media-oriented high-jinks of the sixties. I admit to being one of those in opposition to such tendencies, but I don't recognize myself in your characterization. Indeed, it may well be that the very terms you use to describe the situation are part of the problem, and suggest a continuing misunderstanding of it. For example, it seems likely that words like "radicalism" and "conservatism," "orthodox" and "unorthodox" are no longer appropriate to discussions of modern culture. Originally borrowed from the language of politics and religion, these terms have by now become so freighted with extra-aesthetic meanings as to retain value, in such dialogues as this one, only as a form of invective. They reflect the growing ideological character of criticism in the sixties, a character that developed partly in response to the dwindling options of American politics. This fact was real, and the ideological response was honorably motivated. Still, at the same time that our society was becoming politically closed, it was busting wide open culturally. As a result, it is sentimental to assume that a cultural "radical" can claim quite the same assumptions, frustrations, and apocalyptic vocabulary as a radical in politics.

It should now be sufficiently obvious that the avant-garde movement in America no longer exists in its previous form, and that what passes for "unorthodox" or "radical" culture today is often an extension of Madison Avenue—which is to say, of marketing. "There is a marked suspicion," you write, "of any deviation from the accepted notions of seriousness, as there is of any departure from the orthodox version of the mainstream." One is obliged to ask, What mainstream? What orthodoxy? What accepted notions of seriousness? The image you conjure up here of an embattled group of minority artists trying to survive in the face of a philistine public and a reactionary critical establishment is simply unrecognizable in the seventies; it belongs to the twenties. Today we have a public supine before every cultural novelty, and an army of intellectual critics laboring on behalf of "innovation" side by side with television commentators and the cultural reviewers for the newspapers and mass magazines. In the face of such an alliance, it becomes virtually impossible to identify a "mainstream"; unorthodoxy becomes the new orthodoxy, and fashion the arbiter of taste. What deviations from "accepted notions of seriousness" have been stamped out by hostile "conservative" critics? The Beatles? Camp? Andy Warhol? Abbie Hoffman? Mailer's movies or journalism? Performance groups? Guerrilla theatre? Grotowski? Jean-Luc Godard? Minimal art? John Cage? Each is dutifully tintyped in *Newsweek* and *Time,* interviewed on the Dick Cavett and Merv Griffin shows, and analyzed in depth by serious critics in the pages of intellectual journals. No, the danger today is not from a "marked suspicion" of the unorthodox, but from too ready an acceptance of it. The emblematic avant-garde figure is no longer the expatriate artist, starving and unrecognized in his Paris garret, but rather the upwardly mobile experimental theatre director—catapulted, in the wink of an eye, from the lofts of La Mama to a Broadway stage, where he now peddles nudity, hippie sensationalism, street theatre, and experimental techniques to Broadway audiences at fifteen dollars a ticket, not counting the taxi and baby-sitter.

Given the willingness of virtually everyone, and most especially the mass media, to welcome "new works, new writers, new forms," it is less important for intellectuals to receive the new with the "generosity" you suggest than with discrimination, so as to try to distinguish the truly original from the passing fad. One way to start, perhaps, is to refuse to participate in what remains the authentic American philistinism: anti-intellectualism and hatred of the past. I confess I am a little disturbed to find in your statement the inference that those who find value in "old works" are necessarily clinging to "old values" and "old institutions." This seems to me a break with your own traditionally open cultural position. It was of *Partisan Review* that Lionel Trilling once wrote, in "The Function of the Little Magazine," that "it has wished to accommodate the old and the new, the traditional and the experimental, the religious and the positivistic, the hopeful and the despairing," adding that *PR*'s single abiding standard, by which it conferred unity on diversity, was that of "intelligence and imagination." Had our culture not become so hopelessly addled by politics, I don't think we would need to be reminded that there is continuity between advanced new works and what you call "the culture of the past," or that this continuity is one of our few lines of defense against the indignities and barbarisms of our civilization. By what logic does a love of Shakespeare imply an affirmation of "traditional themes" and "conventional structures"? Isn't it possible to appreciate rock music without asking Beethoven to pack up, or pretending that even the finest folk expressions have an equivalence with the depths and complexities of high art?

It is through the confusion of culture with politics that such misconceptions arise, as critics choose sides on behalf of the new or the old in a contemporary version of the battle between ancients and moderns. But the standard of value in a work of art is not the "radical" or "conservative" view of the artist—which is why your concession about Dostoevsky and Eliot misses the point. Actually, virtually no great modern writers have expressed, in their art, the kind of views you seem to admire, whatever they may have believed as civic men. As Trilling points out in the same essay, "We see that to these writers . . . Proust, Joyce, Lawrence, Eliot, Yeats, Mann (in his creative work), Kafka, Rilke, Gide . . . the liberal ideology has been at best a matter of indifference." Why this is so has something to do with the metaphysical concerns of the artist, something to do with the nondemocratic nature of great art. But to demand liberal or radical or conservative views of artists is to risk losing not only what they have to offer us but, ultimately, what we have to offer them, as beings with an existence beyond our "views."

It is true that younger artists sometimes tend to be contemptuous of the past or try to annihilate their predecessors: this comes from an understandable desire to carve a space for themselves. Still, unless we critics are going to function as publicists, we would do well to avoid imitating this partisanship, particularly since the best artists have usually avoided it. On the subject of the new and the old, the unorthodox and the orthodox, it is still Chekhov who speaks most cogently through the character of his "advanced" writer, Treplev: "I come more and more to realize that it is not a question of new and old forms, but that what matters is that a man should write without thinking of forms at all, write because it springs freely from his soul." This remark, so old-fashioned in its sincerity, breaks strangely on the ears of an age that exalts insincerity, but it rebukes us, nevertheless, with its power and truth.

What I am arguing for, finally, is a truce in the war of the ancients and moderns, and a return to cultural pluralism. One place to start is right in the pages of our intellectual journals. For these journals, as they have ceased to be "little magazines," have grown increasingly narrow and restrictive, attracting along with their larger readerships a certain depressing predictability. Is one in any doubt about how the *New York Review* and *Partisan Review* on the one side, and *Commentary* and the *Public Interest* on the other, would respond on such issues as, say, the youth movement, revisionist history, a book by Angela Davis, the question of pornography and censorship, the essays of George P. Elliott, the education theories of Ivan Illich, or the political writings of Noam Chomsky? Each has developed editorial positions on virtually every book, author, and topic. If this persists, these journals will freeze into glacial postures, commissioning writers who can be confidently expected to argue the house position through reviews and articles, sacrificing intellectual surprise for the sake of ideological consistency. Inevitably, and as a corollary, the number of articles on culture and art has greatly decreased in proportion to those devoted to polemics and politics. It is this, I believe, that presently constitutes a more serious danger to culture than "political and cultural drifts to the right," since it seems to be common to radical and conservative journals alike. (I should add that this symposium is a hopeful sign to me that such monolithic ice floes may be in the process of breaking up.)

Another way to encourage cultural diversity, paradoxically enough, is to reaffirm high standards, leaving the products of the media freaks and the Madison Avenue cowboys to the commodity culture that spawned them. For if there is still any energy or purpose left in cultural radicalism, it is to be found in the defense of artistic values against the exploiters and profiteers, and the application of the most exacting standards, regardless of the "views" of the writer under consideration. In short, what the culture needs most today is not okay opinions and good hearts, not passionate and indiscriminate publicizing of the new, but intelligence and imagination, informed taste, and a revival of faith in the idiosyncratic, redeeming power of great art. (1972)

Freedom and Constraint in the American Theatre

Any account of the state of free expression in the American theatre, however doubtful it is about the future, must be prepared to acknowledge that we are presently enjoying a period of cultural autonomy unique in our history, and probably in the history of the world. It is a peculiar paradox of our age that just when political possibilities have grown considerably circumscribed, artistic possibilities have burst their confines, and our freedom to express ourselves, including our sense of mortification and despair over our political condition, has become virtually unlimited. At the present time, one can put almost anything on the American stage except provocations that lead to mayhem or panic; official censorship is rarely, if ever, exercised; and the public is willing to sit still for representations that a few years ago might have issued in complaints, warrants, or riots. Permissiveness in regard to sexual acts in the theatre has been extended to everything short of actual copulation, and for the first time in almost twenty-five hundred years it is possible to satirize the highest leaders of government on the stage without fear of physical harm or legal retribution.

It is not my intention here to argue the merits of this new freedom. Obviously, it can be used well or badly, depending on the occasion. I think we must be prepared to protect it, regardless of how it is used, at the same time that we should be encouraging its proper employment and cautioning against abuse. Nor am I willing to prophesy whether or not this freedom will last. The recent imprisonment of Ralph Ginsburg, publisher of *Eros,* on charges of mail violation in sending out unsolicited erotic material and the withdrawal by the Public Broadcasting System of Woody Allen's satire on officials of the Nixon administration suggests that fears, pressures, and statutes still exist that may eventually endanger the freedom of the theatre. Rather than prognosticate about the unpredictable future, however, I would prefer to describe the past and the present: to place our theatrical freedom in historical context, to make some effort to account for it, and to suggest what, aside from the omnipresent danger of government intervention, is now inhibiting its healthy expression.

First the history, for our present situation is a very rare one indeed. Most of us are aware that the Athenian comic dramatist Aristophanes enjoyed considerable license, during the time of the demagogue Cleon, to attack the politicians, playwrights, philosophers, and poltroons of his day. Accompanying his social-political commentary—indeed, often informing it—Aristophanes expressed a sexual exuberance through the phallic form of his comedy, and through its concluding *komos* or orgy of song, dance, and lovemaking. Already the parallel with our own time is clear; and it is significant that fifth-century Athens, like contemporary America, was embroiled in a long, brutal, senseless, and spiritually debilitating war, which Aristophanes, like many of our own dramatists, took the opportunity to criticize at the very moment it was failing and his country's military ambitions were being disappointed.

In acknowledging this parallel, we must also acknowledge that it is the only one of its kind in recorded history. Even Athens itself enjoyed this freedom for only a very short period, since, partly in reaction to military defeat, it quickly declined into a tyranny; and a mere quarter of a century after Aristophanes had satirized him in *The Clouds,* Socrates was handed his cup of hemlock "for searching into things," as his judges put it, "under the earth and above the heavens." During the rule of Macedonia, Greek comedy turned soft and romantic, evasive and domestic, avoiding all political reference or erotic playfulness, while the comic theatre of Rome, except for occasional lapses into vitality by Plautus, tended to imitate the prettified escapism of Menandrian comedy.

In the next great period of theatre—the Elizabethan-Jacobean age in England—the kind of freedom enjoyed by Aristophanes was no longer even conceivable. Shakespeare's theatre was hardly genteel, and a certain limited kind of bawdry was acceptable under Elizabethan ground rules, but agencies of the government were ever vigilant about stage entertainments that might contain matter offensive to the crown. When the office of the Master of the Revels was bureaucratized into the office of the Lord Chamberlain, the powers of the censor grew increasingly strict and repressive: a statute only recently repealed in England made it a form of treason to represent living royalty on the stage. Shakespeare's career was in jeopardy for a while because Queen Elizabeth correctly divined analogies between her reign and that of Richard II, after the Earl of Essex commissioned the play *Richard II* upon his return from Ireland to rouse the people in revolt against the Queen. And just a few years later Ben Jonson was imprisoned by James I, and escaped a slit nose only by pleading benefit of clergy, because a play on which he had collaborated contained some criticism of the way the King sold off his knighthoods for a hundred pounds.

Because of the power of agencies of censorship in England and Europe, whether called the Lord Chamberlain, the Académie Française, or the Office of the Inquisition, the relationship of the Western playwright to the political structure was historically that of a flattering importuner to a mighty monarch. Shakespeare extolled the Queen in his comedies and validated her right to the throne in his histories; by creating the roles of the weird sisters in *Macbeth,* he seemed to confirm the prejudices of a king who had recently announced, contrary to growing opinion, that witches really existed. The Spanish dramatist Lope de Vega wrote *The Sheep Well* not to celebrate the democratic unity of a Spanish village, as is mistakenly affirmed sometimes, but rather to defend the powers of the Castilian monarchs against the feudal lords who were challenging their authority. Molière was a sycophant of Louis XIV, and owed his meteoric rise as a playwright, as well as his recovery after the *Tartuffe* controversy, to powerful friends at court. Restoration dramatists made fulsome references, in countless prologues and epilogues, to the wit and wisdom of Charles I. And while Thomas Otway could satirize Shaftesbury in *Venice Preserved,* because the Whig leader had already been arrested for treason, when John Gay attacked a minister still in power in *The Beggar's Opera,* he helped bring on the Licensing Act of 1737, which effectively terminated political reference on the English stage for the next two hundred years.

If the monarchy was repressive of theatrical freedom, the various revolutions that overthrew the monarchy didn't much improve the situation. The Puritan interregnum in England closed the theatres for eighteen years; the French Revolution closed them, too, for a short period, though they were later opened to all comers; and although the Bolshevik Revolution greatly increased the quantity of theatrical activity in Russia, it imposed a censorship even more terrible than before. Indeed, the history of theatre in the modern world can scarcely be called a history of freedom. Totalitarian countries, recognizing the utility of theatre as an instrument of propaganda and indoctrination, also recognized its power as an instrument of subversion, and suppressed, exiled, or executed those who chose to write plays for nontendentious purposes. Stalin may have had the Soviet writer Mayakovsky killed because buried in his propaganda plays were seeds of political satire, while Brecht had to flee Nazi Germany, along with an army of German artists, lest he suffer the same fate at the hands of Hitler.

The record of democratic countries differs in degree rather than kind. Nobody in the West has yet been executed for theatrical deviationism, but Bernard Shaw was fearful enough to withhold *Heartbreak House* from the stage until after World War I because he found truth-telling incompatible with the defense of the realm; the Federal Theatre in America was effectively destroyed by act of Congress because it occasionally criticized acts of Congress; and the theatre that issued from the Allied countries during World War II was an endless charade of official platitudes, patriotic lies, and pious affirmations.

Undoubtedly the most dismal days in the history of our own theatre were the fifties, when the stage, along with movies and television, was subjected to scrutiny by the home-grown yahoos of the House Un-American Activities Committee. Witness after witness was hauled before this sorry tribunal to confess past political errors, to name companions in sin, to testify to the anti-Communist nature of their present work—or else to take refuge under the Fifth Amendment lest they risk imprisonment for contempt of Congress. In this parade of the craven and defiant before the institutionalized philistinism of Cold War America, the very idea of a free theatre seemed to wither and die—effectively destroyed not only by the chauvinism and hostility of the committee itself, but by the abject careerism of those who preferred to scrape before their inquisitors rather than earn a television blackball or sacrifice a Hollywood contract.

Yet so swiftly did the cultural climate change that within ten years this period had come to seem unreal and distant, and a whole new generation was demanding back those rights that had been abdicated. The Eisenhower administration saw the end of the McCarthy era, and the conclusion of the fearful fifties; Kennedy's assassination cast a shadow over the sixties; Johnson was President; and we were mired in the Vietnam war. In response to those various catastrophes, as well as in reaction to the person of Lyndon Johnson himself, American dissent had once again grown strong and vocal—and unlike the previous radicalism, demoralized as it was by Stalinism and the Cold War, it was not to be easily silenced. Simultaneously with the emergence of antiwar protest, America was throwing off its traditional Puritanism. The sixties saw not only political confrontation but confrontation with the laws against erotic movies, books, and plays; and the court cases that resulted usually ended in a rout for censorship and a victory for the forces of freedom. The volume of dissent had managed to blow open the doors and windows of the American theatre.

Perhaps the crucial event in opening up our stage was the off-Broadway production of Barbara Garson's play *MacBird*. A remorseless attack on President Johnson, on the Kennedy family, and on the whole structure of American politics—a satire in pseudo-Shakespearean verse that cast political leaders in the roles of *Macbeth* in order to expose the corrosive lust for power that lies behind the orderly façade of government— *MacBird* was clearly an impudent and vituperative slander, but it had an extraordinary influence and liberating impact on what was to follow. Looking back on it after six years of uninhibited theatrical activity, it is almost impossible to describe how unusual it seemed at the time, and what a singular act of courage it represented. Suffice it to say, it was a work without a precedent. Written as an underground pamphlet, sold under the counter at bookstores, read aloud at protest rallies and antiwar meetings (I myself gave portions of the play their first New York hearing during a teach-in at Columbia in 1966), *MacBird* had arguable value as a literary work, and no value at all as an interpretation of history, but it nevertheless proved a liberating event for American theatre, as *Dr. Strangelove* had been for the American film, Lenny Bruce for American comedy, and *Catch-22* for American literature. For all its malice and extremism, despite the fact that it probably embodied and inspired considerable irresponsibility, *MacBird* made it possible at last for the performing arts to use those freedoms guaranteed by but rarely exercised under the Bill of Rights.

Many of us who had lived through the McCarthy days were certain that *MacBird* would never be produced or, if produced, would be severely harassed by the authorities. The play was too offensive, not only to Johnson conservatives but to Kennedy liberals as well. Yet *MacBird* went on to enjoy a long, uninterrupted run at the Village Gate in New York, as well as inspiring innumerable performances on campuses and in cities throughout the nation, and stimulating a whole new era of political satire. (Philip Roth's book *Our Gang* and de Antonio's film *Millhouse* are only two of its descendants.) It was also partly responsible for a succession of antiwar plays, beginning with the crude but well-intentioned *Viet Rock*, and it had some impact on the emergence of guerrilla theatre. Contemporary with these manifestations came an era of black protest plays, frequently obscene and often abusive, and a period of theatrical nudity and pornography, beginning with works like *Dionysus in '69, Futz, Oh! Calcutta,* and *The Dirtiest Show in Town.* With liberation in fashion, homosexuality, long a taboo subject on the American stage, was now being openly treated in plays like *The Boys in the Band,* while the homosexual playwright who failed to declare his sexual preferences in his work was being made an object of derision in *Nightride,* and even in the theatre pages of the *New York Times.*

Undoubtedly, the culmination of the new political and sexual emphasis could be found in the visit of the Living Theatre during 1968 and 1969, when spectators were invited onto the stage to copulate with the actors or into the streets, after the performance, to liberate prisons and free the prisoners. Theatrical freedom, in short, had become so open and manifest that it was now becoming synonymous with action, while the theatrical occasion was becoming an opportunity for anarchic gestures and total abandon. Indeed, so fast were things happening that even the Living Theatre failed to keep pace. At one performance of *Paradise Now,* after the bikini-clad actors announced they were not allowed to take their clothes off, members of the audience stripped down to the buff, while others, replying to the actors' plaint that they weren't allowed to smoke marijuana, lit up and filled the theatre with pot fumes. It was on this threshold, when the possibilities of freedom were outstripping even the theatre's capacity to imagine them, that one felt a conscious drawing back, and a nostalgia for more sublimative forms of performance. The intoxication brought on by unleashed hostility, acting out, public orgy, and romantic confession had begun to wear off, and in the sober morning light it became more apparent that theatrical freedom did not have to mean replacing the artist with the spectator or the work of art with the spontaneous act. The Living Theatre visit had performed an unintentional service by marking the territory beyond which it was fruitless and unproductive to tread.

This is where we find the theatre at the present moment, enjoying an unprecedented freedom in political and sexual matters, its major censorship battles won, its enemies routed, its audiences unshockable, its rights and privileges unlimited. And the question I would raise now is, if everything is so marvelous why is the theatre so demoralized? Why do those who work in the profession often seem so despondent? Why is it now so difficult to arouse enthusiasm even for the most imaginative and experimental work? Why do audiences frequently seem so torpid and performers so listless?

To say that we lack plays and playwrights is not really to answer these questions. It is true that nobody writing for the theatre today has O'Neill's stature, or even that of Williams and Miller; it is also true that we have never before had such a large number of good young writers with serious ambitions. Sam Shepard, Ronald Ribman, Maria Irene Fornes, Terrence McNally, David Rabe, Rochelle Owens, Michael Weller, Charles Dizenzo, Rosalyn Drexler—these are the names of playwrights of talent, imagination, and intensity. None has written a major play—some may never write a major play— but the encouraging thing is the quality of their shared ambition, their search for an authentic poetic vision. Each year, two or three names can be removed from such a list for not having realized their promise, but two or three new names can be added as well, for the time has come when young writers are being attracted to the theatre as an important literary form, instead of as a potential financial bonanza. In short, as the American theatre has lost its commercial appeal, it has gained in its potential for artistry, and the talent that exists is now being used for serious purposes, and not just to manufacture Broadway hits.

Along with the growing number of serious playwrights, we at last have a growing number of serious theatres. No longer is the fate of a play tied to the whims of the commercial producer who makes his decisions, chooses his cast and director, and asks for revisions primarily on the basis of what will sell. Resident companies are mushrooming throughout the country, supported partially by the community, partially by foundations, partially by the National Endowment for the Arts, always precariously balanced financially, but still not completely dependent on the box office for their survival: these are geared to offer the right kind of hospitality to new plays. The Mark Taper Forum in Los Angeles, the Arena Stage in Washington, the Public Theatre in New York, the Yale Repertory Theatre and the Long Wharf in New Haven, the Chelsea Theatre in Brooklyn, the Trinity Square Playhouse in Providence, the Open Theatre, the Magic Theatre, the Manhattan Project, Café La Mama, and countless others are all devoted to seeking out, commissioning, and producing the best available plays, often with actors, directors, and designers who have already worked together as an ensemble.

So we don't lack theatres, either, though the traditional centers on Broadway and off-Broadway don't seem to be holding, indeed are falling apart. What do we lack, then, if the material exists, along with the necessary producing units and the freedom to do it honestly and well? I would suggest that we lack a passionate engagement between the theatre and its actual or potential public. Americans, at the moment, just don't seem capable of an open and energetic response to the theatre's special powers. I would further suggest that the apathetic, indifferent relationship between the spectator and the stage is one of the major reasons why the theatre is now able to enjoy such unusual freedom from resentment, constraint, and interference.

What I am saying is that the theatre has achieved its freedom at the very moment when it has become rather hollow, that the facile way in which even the most revolutionary theatrical expressions are being absorbed is the clearest proof that they are having no effect. This idea, with its suggestions of repressive tolerance, may sound Marcusian. But unlike Herbert Marcuse, I see no conspiracies behind this dilemma, no conscious plan to stifle dissent by assimilating it—merely a combination of forces and accidents that have helped to create a cultural atmosphere inhospitable to real theatrical connection. One of these is the increasing sophistication of the audiences. If the theatre is suffering from its very security, if nobody feels particularly threatened even by its most radical twists and turns, then this may be because we have grown so jaundiced and skeptical that the theatre has lost its power to reach us.

Certainly the day seems to be over when, like Claudius in *Hamlet,* a guilty person sitting at a play could be moved to proclaim his malefactions, or could be infuriated enough, like that legendary Texan watching a touring production of *Othello,* to shoot the actor playing Iago for his villainy. When the Abbey Theatre first produced Synge's *Playboy of the Western World,* the spectators rioted over what they called a libel on the Irish character, giving the poet Yeats an opportunity to denounce them from the stage and later to write a brilliant denunciatory poem on the occasion. When David Rabe's *Sticks and Bones* opened at the Public Theatre, it was approvingly received by both audiences and critics, and transferred to Broadway, even though it could more accurately be called a libel on a national character, particularly on the character of the middle-class audiences supporting it. It is obvious which of these two audiences is the more tolerant, but which is the more alive? Clearly, the Irish took their theatre seriously, and we do not; they were jealous of their national reputation, and we are not; they could engage themselves emotionally with what they saw on stage, and we cannot. The Irish may have reacted to their artists ferociously, blindly, stupidly, but they reacted with the animation of living men.

If the history of the modern theatre is one of mutual suspicion between the playwright and his audience, the history of the post-modern theatre here in America is one of quick rewards and instant media replay, where the serious writer fights not poverty and neglect but the fickleness of a culture that picks him up and discards him before he has had sufficient time to develop properly. Like any jaded culture, we hunger not for experience but for novelty, while an army of media commentators labors ceaselessly to identify something new.

One of the causes of this condition can be found in the peculiar relationship between the American playgoer and the American theatre critic: never before has a handful of reviewers possessed so much power and lacked so much authority. The mediocrity of newspaper and television reviewing throughout the country is nothing new; it is the inevitable result, first, of the need for haste and, second, of choosing reviewers from the ranks of journalism (from the sports page, say, or from the dance columns) rather than from literary or professional training grounds. What is new, and most depressing, is the scarcity of decent critics anywhere else. It is almost as if the theatre had been abandoned by men and women of intelligence and taste, and delivered over wholesale to the publicists, the proselytizers, and the performers.

Theatrical criticism once attracted writers of the caliber of Stark Young, Eric Bentley, Mary McCarthy, Elizabeth Hardwick, Wilfrid Sheed, Richard Hayes, Richard Gilman, Susan Sontag, Kenneth Tynan—writers, in short, who could be expected to analyze a play or production intelligently, and to correct the misjudgments of the daily press. When in 1959 Jack Gelber's *The Connection* was savaged by the daily newspapers, it was salvaged through the combined support of the weekly magazines, just as, three years earlier, the intellectual critics rehabilitated the American reputation of *Waiting for Godot* after its disastrous reception at the hands of such reviewers as Walter Kerr. (The process used to work the other way, too: in 1958, Archibald MacLeish's *J.B.* was more harshly evaluated by the magazine critics after the *New York Times* called it "one of the most memorable works of the century.") Today this kind of corrective has largely disappeared, as the dissenting critics have departed or changed their focus. Most intellectual journals don't even include theatre chronicles any more. Harold Clurman still holds down a corner of the *Nation,* but his writing has grown fatigued and his judgments flaccid. Stanley Kauffmann writes too irregularly about the theatre in the *New Republic* to have much impact. And John Simon's virtually single-handed crusade, in *New York* magazine, to preserve high standards has become vitiated by his uncontrolled savagery, his punning style, his peculiar prejudices, his personal attacks on the physical appearance of actors, and his obsessive campaign against real or imagined homosexuality on the stage.

Simon's progress may suggest why so many other serious writers have abandoned theatre criticism, for it shows what may happen to a man of intelligence and discrimination when he observes too long the execrable products of the American theatrical scene. First, he becomes so enraged over what he sees that he gets carried away on a wave of aggression; then, he gets locked into his fury and turns it into a mode of performance; and finally, he gets picked up by the mass media to play the role of Mr. Nasty Badman for the amusement of the television audience.

As for the young, who would normally be expected to swell the ranks of serious theatre critics, providing new energy, insight, and commitment, they seem peculiarly indifferent to the profession—partly because they have lost interest in the theatre itself for the moment, partly because they distrust what they call "élitist" standards of excellence, but mostly, I would guess, because they have no exciting models to imitate. For while there is nothing like an exemplary critic to generate enthusiasm for the practice of criticism, the fact is that very few writers on the theatre are setting very good examples these days. The *Village Voice* stable seems to share the same reflexive enthusiasm for every spasm of the post-modern imagination, while black theatre critics engage in a similar kind of proselytizing on behalf of black theatre, proclaiming the death of Western drama every time Imamu Baraka or Ed Bullins delivers another assault on the honkies. Even Jack Kroll of *Newsweek* has begun using his considerable sophistication in praise of second-rate plays, perhaps hoping to stimulate a flagging interest in the theatre by inflating the reputations of budding black and avant-garde playwrights.

In the face of such obvious partisanship, the reader can begin to lose his trust in the sincerity of the reviewer, and nowhere is this insincerity revealed more patently than in the columns of Clive Barnes. Barnes's writing for the *New York Times* combines a transparent lack of respect for the American theatre with a manifest compulsion to save it from economic disaster. This results in a style compounded of such glaring contradictions that it is often difficult to parse two consecutive sentences without falling into confusion. Barnes's notorious characterization of Odets's *The Country Girl* as "precisely the kind of gorgeous mediocrity we need on Broadway" is only the most famous example of his bewildering ambivalence. About the place in which the play was produced, he wrote: "The Eisenhower theatre, the most anonymous, blandest, and nicest constituent of Washington's new, awful, and efficient Kennedy Center . . ." *Rain* he called "a gloriously bad play . . . a very considerable monument to a type of theatre now dead—ridiculous but full-blooded." Of another Broadway play, he said, "*A Conflict of Interest* is one of those classic American political melodramas that not only are totally incredible but, remarkably enough, partly believable." And incredibly believable as it may seem, he documented his enthusiasm for *That Championship Season* by proclaiming, "It takes American drama back to Paddy Chayefsky, which is not the same thing as taking it back to Albee, Williams or O'Neill, but is still progress in the right direction."

Progress backward is not the only contortion to which Barnes's style subjects the reader—nor are his contradictions limited only to single reviews. Barnes may change his mind about a play between the first and second time he sees it, without any acknowledgment that his previous opinion has altered. In a notice of the Long Wharf production of Robert Anderson's *Solitaire/Double Solitaire* in New Haven, for ex-

ample, Barnes grew so ecstatic about the work that, largely on
the basis of his endorsement, it was invited first to the Edin-
burgh Festival, where it met generally sour reviews, and thence
to Broadway, where it received a cold reception—even from
Mr. Barnes. The same production that in March he called
Robert Anderson's "finest achievement to date . . . one of those
nights when you feel proud and good about the American
theatre" had by the following October become for him something with "more of the scent of the theatre about it than the
breath of life," tricked out by "one of the best exponents of
the boulevard play." It closed in seven weeks.

Related to this, and suggested by it, is the trope I have come
to think of as the Barnes Hyperbolic. Perhaps in recognition
that the *Times* is now the single arbitrator of success or failure
in the commercial theatre, Barnes has begun resorting to
greater and greater extravagances of style in order to suggest
that he has any enthusiasm at all for a play—with the result
that he is in process of losing his credibility entirely with the
theatregoing public.*

It is difficult to take seriously the judgments of a man who
can speak in nothing but superlatives—who, in the course of a
single year, says five or six different actors are giving the most
brilliant performance of their lives, calls eight or ten resident
companies one of the finest in the country, announces four or
five plays to be the best of this or any season, compares a
young writer who has just completed his first play with the
mature Chekhov, and identifies Stacy Keach as the finest
American Hamlet since Barrymore, though he is too young to
have seen Barrymore's performance and is very likely unfamiliar with most of the American Hamlets that followed.
Barnes's use of hyperbole, with its promiscuous display of the
word "best," exposes not the splendors of the theatre season
but rather its bankruptcy, for it suggests that Barnes's need
to identify works of merit or interest has far outrun the

* By contrast, Walter Kerr, writing in the Sunday section of the *Times*
(having voluntarily abandoned his power as a daily reviewer), has been
gaining in credibility, though not in influence, by virtue of his forth-
rightness and candor—though he still strikes me as very limited in his
vision of the theatre.

theatre's capacity to create them.* Needless to say, after the seventh or eighth time that a spectator has found himself misled by such language, either cynicism or apathy is bound to set in, with the result that Barnes is developing the capacity to break but not to make a play, and even those works for which he presumably has some genuine feeling (the Broadway production of Michael Weller's *Moonchildren,* for example) are no longer able to attract audiences on the basis of his reviews.

Obviously, no theatre can benefit in the long run from fake approval, partly because the critic becomes discredited, partly because the spectator grows disenchanted, partly because the theatre practitioner begins to lose faith in his craft. The very rare work with serious aspirations gets lost in the general atmosphere of praise—either because it is ignored or unappreciated or because it is acclaimed in the same way as everything else. When the inspired and the routine are treated exactly alike, the act of criticism comes to seem arbitrary and capricious; when the corrective impulse is abandoned, the whole construct of standards breaks down. A serious literary artist can always hope for an understanding review or two in the midst of the general incomprehension, and anyway, regardless of reviews, his book continues to exist for future generations to discover. But the theatre artist writes on air, and preserves his work only in the memories of those who see it. In the present critical atmosphere, even those memories are tainted. The marriage that must exist in any art form between the mind that creates and the mind that responds has begun to dissolve in the theatre, with the result that the art form itself is in danger of losing its purpose and direction.

Meanwhile the theatre artist is foundering in a sea of approval where he finds no walls against which to press, no

* This is not to say that Barnes praises everything. As a matter of perverse fact, he often seems enraged by any display of intellect in the theatre: witness his hatred of the plays of Bernard Shaw and his unremitting attacks on the highly original, idiosyncratic productions of Jonathan Miller. Given his eagerness to find merit even in the most dreadful theatrical products, it is hard not to conclude that Barnes's rare dislikes are motivated by other than aesthetic considerations.

barriers to break, no limitations to transcend—only an escalating praise of his work by critics who don't really mean it, coupled with the inattention of spectators who don't really care. As children are sometimes driven wild by their failure to provoke an overly tolerant parent, so this theatre artist may find such approval, though flattering at first, enfeebling to his will, confusing to his sense of purpose, maddening to his spirit. And he may find, too, that like the child with the permissive parent, he is not really cared about in some profound way, that he is regarded as an abstraction rather than a living creature, that he is failing to make a truly human connection. And the result is that his frustrations lead him into ever greater provocations in the misguided hope that someone at last will pay some serious attention.

What has this to do with freedom of expression in the theatre? Everything. For at the very moment when true freedom has at last become possible, after years of timidity, censorship, and inhibition, there may be nobody around capable of enjoying it. It is as if an orator, dumb all his life, were about to open his mouth and discourse the rarest speech —except that all his auditors have fallen asleep. One almost begins to think with nostalgia of the time when the theatre had the capacity to offend the government, bring on the watch-and-ward societies, call down the police, infuriate the critics, make mad the guilty and appal the free—because those very threats to its freedom were a testimony to its powers. If the theatre wishes to retain these powers, it must demand a criticism that is informed and exacting, and seek out a spectator with an independent mind. It must be prepared to sacrifice praise for the sake of discrimination, and acceptance for the sake of vitality. It is not, in short, the theatre that must be freed now, but those who observe it—free to judge, to respond, to develop a passionate relationship to the stage. Without this, I fear, freedom in the theatre will remain a mockery, an empty option of the mute and the deaf.   (1972)

2
Home Thoughts from Abroad

A Tale of Two Cities

With the exception of a fouled-up telephone system, all services designed for the public seem to be superior in London: transportation (remarkably comfortable and convenient); the police (consistently courteous and helpful); health plans (government subsidized, expertly staffed); the parks (spacious, clean, safe, ablaze with flowers); and, of course, the theatre. Looking back on our own disintegrating services, one begins to see a correspondence between civic virtues and the communal arts. Where the society is brutish, anarchic, apathetic, opportunistic, the theatre will soon begin to reflect those qualities, as it does now in New York. Where the society is gentle, civilized, unthreatening, and people-centered, the theatre will reflect that, too, as it does here in London. S. J. Perelman recently returned to New York, after a brief expatriation, complaining that one can have quite enough of "couth." It is easy to see what he means. Still, although the excessive gentility of the English upper classes makes private conversation rather forced and individual creation a little inhibited, the public life of this city is a blessed tonic after the nastiness of the American urban nightmare. And there is nothing quite like being in a London theatre audience, sharing that almost forgotten sense of electric anticipation in front of a rising curtain.

Theatre is essential to the life of this city, and one finds it everywhere. Just as every major city in England has its own thriving repertory company, so there is interesting theatre to be found in every borough and district of London. Yes, the West End still survives, its theatres clustered around Shaftesbury Avenue in the manner of a more respectable, less dangerous Broadway. But decentralization urges the theatregoer away from the conventional amusement areas—to the Bankside in Southwark, where Sam Wanamaker is creating another Globe Theatre and where the National Theatre company is building its new home; to the Aldwych, where the Royal Shakespeare Company makes its London headquarters; to Sloane Square, where the Royal Court still holds sway, with an additional theatre upstairs to house experimental troupes; to the Stratford district, where Joan Littlewood conducts her Theatre Workshop; to Euston, where Michael Croft runs his vigorous National Youth Theatre in a brand-new house; and, most curiously, to the innumerable pubs in every section of London, where the Fringe theatre groups perform both at lunchtime and at night, in tiny rooms on minimal stages.

I make no comment on the quality of these theatres, which range from awful to marvelous, but rather on the fact that they offer plays of every possible description—commercial and avant-garde, in repertory and *en suite,* author-written and group-improvised, political and aesthetic, popular and arcane —in an abundant outpouring of activity that keeps the reviewer running and the spectator spent. What strikes me as remarkable is how essentially noncompetitive all this is, how little threatened one theatre is by the success of another, how spacious is the theatrical world of a single city. Oh, rivalries exist, of course—between the National Theatre and the Royal Shakespeare Company, for example, or between the Young Vic and the National Youth Theatre—but these seem inspired less by competition for audiences than by competition for grants from the Arts Council, which subsidizes, to a greater or lesser extent, almost every permanent theatre of consequence in England. Indeed, the amount of these subsidies accounts largely for the accessibility and number of these theatres, but if the auditoriums of London, in contrast with New York's half-empty houses, are usually filled, it is not just because ticket prices are lower, but because people go to the theatre here as a habitual part of their daily lives.

There is, as a result, little of that scratching for audiences through expensive publicity and massive subscription campaigns that one finds so frequently in America. There is, besides, little of that familiar, vaguely condescending, educationalist compulsion to awaken the masses to the glories of the drama. (Arnold Wesker used to try to get people out of the pubs and into the theatres; now the very opposite seems to have happened, with people going to theatres in pubs.) Like the BBC, which is providing a great variety of programs to satisfy every taste, the theatre now has something for everybody, and anyone who wishes to see a play has the opportunity to go.

In this sense, England is presently a considerably more pluralistic society than America, since it makes much more allowance for different temperaments and styles. In this quasi-Socialist country, distinctions among people continue to exist in regard to birth and wealth as well, where class lines are still impenetrable and where, if my informants are accurate, 10 percent of the people control 83 percent of the wealth. But if England's class hierarchies are rigid, its cultural hierarchies are extremely flexible: working-class aesthetes are no more unusual than upper-class philistines. This is hardly to say that the average level of taste is any higher here than it is anywhere else, but rather that the average is not allowed to predominate. English culture is remarkable for the way in which it continues to offer choices.

I find this an infinitely more healthy and desirable situation than now obtains in America, where consensus rule virtually dictates the options of aesthetic experience and anything that cannot immediately collect an audience is looked upon with suspicion and distrust. In such a situation, leadership in the arts gradually passes from the creator to the consumer, and the culture tends to get flattened down to the level of the lowest common denominator. The basest example of this can be found in the quality of American television programs, almost all of which seem to have been produced by the same faceless people for the benefit of the same characterless mass. It can also be observed in the way a given community can decide the fate of its resident theatre on the basis of audience ratings and civic support.

Such numerical arguments account for the notion in America that the theatre is dying because it lacks the popular appeal of the movies. (It may well be dying, but hardly for that reason.) This creates a kind of defensiveness in theatre people that sometimes takes the form of "democrateering," as Eric Bentley once called it—the tendency of critics and producers to be satisfied with nothing less than a play that appeals to everybody. The inevitable analogy is with Shakespeare, the popular artist *par excellence*; but the trouble with this analogy is that Shakespeare did not write for a debased mass society, and that geniuses of his range and variety unfortunately tend to materialize no more often than once every two thousand years. Indeed, what "democrateering" produces rather more often than *Hamlet* and *Lear* are harmless diversions like the American musical or, in the case of serious works, plays that confirm rather than question the prejudices of their audiences.

That this is true regardless of whether these audiences are radical, black, or middle American suggests that our current theatrical populism is more a political than a cultural phenomenon, designed less for individuals than for constituencies. As a result, we begin to find some American theatre critics evaluating a theatrical work not on the basis of its intrinsic merits but rather on its value to a political movement or an emerging class. In England, on the other hand, highbrow, middlebrow, and lowbrow can co-exist without threat or danger to the other; and although, say, BBC 2 and Radio 3 are often the butt of humor for their *recherché* programing, nobody would think to question the size of their special audiences or the value of their high cultural offerings.

In this way, the English manage to be homogeneous without being homogenized, and unified without being uniform—while we, for all our ethnic diversity, follow ineluctably the path to conformity. Their natural thrust is toward individuality, even eccentricity; ours is toward a magnetic center that will mold all the scattered fragments into a single nuclear mass. Is there any significance in the fact that London has over ten newspapers criticizing theatre while New York, in effect, has only one? The consequences of such variety are certainly clear: no single reviewer, not even a group of reviewers, has the power of life and death over any production; divided notices mean that a play can still survive; and only unanimous critical disapproval can seriously curtail its run.

In short, English culture is in a healthy state, nowhere more so than in the London theatre. This theatre exists not as a status symbol for the middle classes or a soporific for the masses; it serves no particular identity needs for any racial or ethnic groups; it is not a snob center for the upper classes or a special sanctuary for academics and intellectuals—yet, given its variety, I suppose it could also be any of these things discontinuously. It exists, in other words, for people—not *the people,* which is to say, some amorphous abstraction to be hypnotized with idiot diversions or manipulated with stirring slogans—but *people,* in all their manifold diversity, idiosyncratic demands, and measureless breadth. That is why theatre in London is flourishing while in New York it seems to be buckling at the knees. (1972)

Two Plays About Ireland

Richard's Cork Leg and *The Ballygombeen Bequest*

Two plays about Ireland, approximately a decade apart, suggest how deeply the ideological struggles of the intervening years may have altered the life of the theatre.

Richard's Cork Leg was begun by Brendan Behan in 1961, and left unfinished at his death in 1964. Now reconstructed and completed by Alan Simpson, the director of the Abbey Theatre's production at the Royal Court, it seems almost old-fashioned in its irrepressible animal spirits. Behan's gifts as a dramatist were no more orderly than his life as a drunkard. What emerges most vividly from his plays is the jocular-querulous, clamorous-melodious atmosphere of a Dublin pub. *Richard's Cork Leg* has all the theatrical significance of a pint of ale—sometimes full of yeasty ferment, sometimes merely full of boozy conviviality. An amiable shambles, the evening is nevertheless brimming with pleasure, overflowing with good-natured, bubbling zip.

It is typical of the shiftlessness of the work that its epony-mous hero never appears. He is, in fact, mentioned only once in passing when one of the characters, a whore named Rose of Lima, tells of a former husband whose leg was shot off by the British. When they first went to bed together, Rose felt the cork replacement and, not knowing what it was, said daunt-lessly, "Give us a glass of water and I'll chance it." This tone of goofy incontinence is matched only by the play's extravagant characters and setting. Located primarily in a Dublin ceme-tery, it is populated with Behan's familiar *personae* of loqua-cious prostitutes, nubile maidens, puritanical Protestants, phony blind men, Irish revolutionaries and Fascists, and a black mortician, on loan from California's Forest Lawn, who specializes in singing corpses.

As usual, the author compensates for his lack of plot by substituting rhetoric and wit, comic seductions, drunken par-ties, hoary jokes, and a large number of songs, most of them written by Behan to a variety of folk and classical tunes, and performed by a quintet called the Dubliners on a variety of stringed instruments.

The only organizing principle in this gallimaufry is the presence of death, which still retains its customary sting-aling-aling: sex and death (seductions occur on top of gravestones); wealth and death (one corpse is "poxy with money," but as Rose says, "He can kiss my royal Irish arse for all the good his money will do for him now"); science and death ("Go easy with your experiments," cautions a corpse, "or you'll be seeing me sooner than you expect"); and, above all, death and revolutionary politics. For Behan, who saw a bit of such action himself, "graveyards and patriots always go together," and very frequently the innocent get pushed below the turf as well. In the climax of the play, one character mistakenly re-ceives a fusillade intended for a revolutionary; and although he pops up immediately (in typical Behan fashion) for a post-mortem finale, his future singing career, as well as his capacity to drink and fornicate, has been sadly terminated.

The production is quite brilliant, directed with headlong energy and impeccably acted, especially by Joan O'Hara and Eilene Colgan, as the two whores, and Luke Kelly and Ronnie

Drew, as the two ersatz blind men. (Drew sings six of the songs, snapping a hoarse bass-baritone at the tunes like a bullwhip.) A fine memorial to its dead author's love of life, *Richard's Cork Leg* is also an almost anachronistic celebration of unconditioned man—mortal, fallible, self-preserving, yet vivid in his whiskey-soaked humanity.

The Ballygombeen Bequest, written by John Arden in collaboration with his wife, Margaretta D'Arcy, proceeds by similar theatrical means—vaudeville techniques, character cartoons, farcical scenes, folk songs, and jigs—but its ends are, by contrast, quite chillingly inhuman. At least it seemed so to me, though I confess I am usually frozen out by plays about abstractions, even such worthy abstractions as Equality and Justice. Written partly in couplets, this piece concerns an absentee British landlord with a property in Connaught who exploits the labor of his tenant farmer and eventually cheats him out of his squatter's rights on the land. Arden and D'Arcy are considerably exercised by the growing commercialization of rural Irish territory, a condition they attribute to the foreign capitalist ("The man with the long purse that spreads his feet across the land") in cahoots with the Irish Church and the conservative government of John Lynch. The inevitable victims of this exploitation are the Irish laboring classes ("We are the people and the land belongs to us"), who are invariably too innocent to escape the grasping talons of their wily oppressors.

The people, however, grow in aggressive resolve when the second part of the play (covering the years 1957 to 1971) dramatizes how easily exploitation can turn into murder. The British landlord, plagued by a petition designed to return the property to the dead farmer's family, falsely informs British intelligence that the son is harboring terrorists. The young man is captured and, in a particularly harrowing scene, is tortured to death by the police. Like a Behan character, he is momentarily resurrected, rising from his flag-draped coffin to sing a final song, as well as to squeeze the testicles of his enemies; and, as in a Behan finale, the play ends in mayhem, with the cast throwing pies and eating paper money. This is kind of fun, but the pranks are ultimately elbowed aside by the propaganda as the dead boy vows an end to oppression through the militant action of his class ("There are more of us than there is of them").

The disposition of these playwrights to assign vices and virtues exclusively along class lines is admittedly a little archaic—nowadays such divisions are more frequently also racial and generational—but aside from that, the play is perfectly up-to-date in its inclination to substitute caricatures for characters, to select anecdotes that prove a propaganda point, to offer the violence of people's power as an antidote to the violence of the establishment, and to preach to the converted, confirming them in their traditional prejudices. (The night I saw the work, excellently performed by the 7:84 Theatre company before a predominantly Irish audience in Shepherd's Bush, it was received with the fervor of an Agincourt harangue.) Still, are revolutionary clarions the business of the theatre artist? Is the playwright once again going to sacrifice intellectual surprise for the sake of ideological consistency, and thrust a clenched-fist politics in the supple face of unmediated truth and complex reality?

Arden's work, much of which I admire, has always been generous and pacific in its temper; but, like the later O'Casey and the middle Brecht, he now runs the risk of fouling his decent intentions with the emotional imperialism of ideology. *The Ballygombeen Bequest* has been called Arden's first agitprop play: I personally hope it is his last. With such work, he is no longer contributing to art but rather to what George Orwell called "the smelly little orthodoxies that are nowadays contending for our souls." (1972)

Art in an Age of Ideology
England's Ireland

To judge from my own coign of vantage, the minds of serious theatre people in England are presently preoccupied largely with the Irish question. Four recent openings have confronted this subject either directly or in passing, the most recent being an episodic collage by seven playwrights called *England's Ireland*. I find it virtually impossible to exercise the task of dramatic criticism in regard to such a work. It is impudently, if somewhat screechingly, performed, and it possesses occasional satiric deftness—as, for example, in a ritual enacted by a group of Orangemen in derbies who piss in sanctified pots and then drink "the water of the English ascendancy." To evaluate the theatrical qualities of the evening, however, would be to scant the important political issues it raises; and to discuss the issues would be beyond my jurisdiction as a foreign visiting critic.

But then I come from a country with serious troubles of its own, which often find theatrical expression in similar ways, so rather than try to review *England's Ireland,* I would prefer to make some generalizations about why I find plays of this sort so disheartening and, ultimately, so subversive of the very causes they hope to advance. I admit a prejudice here—against the use of theatre as an instrument of social or political utility and, particularly, as an arm of propaganda. I am old enough to remember not only the manipulative lies of Goebbels during World War II but also of our own side when, in order to accelerate the war effort, plays and movies asked us to regard all Japanese and Germans as subhuman, and to consider the wholesale slaughter of the enemy as an occasion for rejoicing. I don't think anyone has yet measured the damage wrought to our spirits by such characterizations, not to mention the appalling dullness forced on our minds; but I know they made Hiroshima possible, and I suspect they paved the way for Vietnam.

England's Ireland proceeds from a similar kind of impulse, particularly when it identifies the British torture-murder of a young Irish boy with the crucifixion of Christ but makes the killing of an English soldier an occasion for comedy. When an Irish revolutionary in this play says, "You have to blow people apart to get them to listen to you," I am reminded of nothing so much as the remark of an American military officer in Vietnam to the effect that "we had to destroy the village in order to save it." Both are perfect examples of what Edmund Wilson once called "the self-assertive sounds" man utters "when he is fighting and swallowing others." But such cant in dramatic form is especially repulsive because it implicates the theatre, which should aspire to the truth, in a conscious act of falsehood.

I do not mean to imply for a moment that the theatre ought to avoid the pressing issues of the time, or even that the playwright should remain scrupulously neutral. But if an artist has developed an adversary position through his perception of a complicated reality, he has the obligation, if he has the power, to deliver this reality back through his art so the audience can reach its own conclusions. This was the way of Shaw; it was usually the way of Brecht; it is the way of every dramatist who has the humanity to keep the ideological animal in him at bay. Aristotle believed that dramatic poetry was superior to history because it has the capacity to render not only the surface of particular events, which taken alone are often lies, but also the universal texture of probable human motive. Understanding such motives may not make immediate converts to a cause, but it permits the spectator to make his judgments in an atmosphere of free inquiry, and thereby creates the possibility of more lasting conversions.

There is, for example, a play still to be written about Northern Ireland, but it would be a tragedy, not a melodrama. It would look with horror on British internment camps, torture practices, the persecution of the Catholic minority, and the perpetuation of a divided Ireland; it would look with equal horror on the indiscriminate bombing of civilians by the provisional wing of the IRA, not to mention its vicious abuse of Catholic women who fraternize with Protestants or English soldiers. It would try to understand the dilemma of a British government apparently eager to disengage itself from a profitless trouble spot but obliged to protect the security of its nationals. And it would press back to the early imperial crime against the Irish people by England, which, like the original sin of American slavery, mocks all the good intentions of a later day, like some modern curse on the house of Atreus.

This play has yet to be conceived. What we have in its

place are simple-minded oppositions, stirring heroics, and the discharge of hate in a righteous cause. And what worries me most about these plays is their aggressiveness, for this leads one to believe that if the Irish question had never existed, certain English writers would have felt compelled to invent it. Aggressiveness of this kind is a quality that permeates a variety of agitprop plays—whether about blacks, Vietnam, or capitalism—where, regardless of the virtue of the cause, it seems to precede its source and linger independently of its stimuli, like monoxide fumes in an empty garage. Freud, whose sweet reason is presently in eclipse, was convinced that if such aggression were not creatively channeled, it would eventually destroy the human race. He never dreamed that the artist, for whom he had such hope and respect, would begin to help the bloody butchers at their work.   (1972)

Reflections on Privacy

Freedom of expression and the laws of libel, the public good versus the rights of the individual, English privacy and American surveillance—these were some of the thoughts that ran through my mind when I was almost prevented, recently, from reviewing a play because it was the object of a threatened lawsuit. The work in question was *The Ballygombeen Bequest,* by John Arden and his wife, Margaretta D'Arcy.

The most remarkable thing about the play is that it is supposed to be based on actual characters; indeed, the program supplies us with the name, address, and telephone numbers of the alleged culprit, presumably in the hope that we will harass the fellow a little. And although the authors amplify the anecdote into an indictment of the middle classes, British capitalism, the Catholic Church, and the conservative government of Jack Lynch, their supporters defend the agitprop simplicities of the work on the grounds of its presumed authenticity. Things like this actually happen, we are reminded, and it is the duty of all right-minded people to protest injustice by applauding the play.

I preferred to withhold my applause, but I was almost forced to withhold my review as well. And what interests me —while we wait for the courts to help decide on the accuracy of the charges—is how much restraint is imposed on English journalism (including drama criticism) by pending litigation. The laws of libel apparently apply not only to those responsible for the original imputations but to any reporter who repeats them. For this reason, *The Ballygombeen Bequest* was largely ignored by the newspapers at the time it opened, and my own notice was allowed to appear in the *Observer* only because it contained no mention of the play's alleged origin in real events.

To one who comes from a country whose libel laws are relatively loose, this kind of journalistic caution comes as something of a surprise; clearly, the English press has limits that would not be tolerated in America. Just a week ago, to cite a recent example, the courts awarded three thousand pounds to a woman reporter who had sued the satirical journal *Private Eye* for suggesting that, in order to gain her information, she had slept around with several politicians, including Harold Wilson. (The courts ignored the magazine's claim that its charge was not serious, though this defense seemed plausible enough considering the plaintiff's matronly appearance and age.) As a further illustration still, the playwright Rolf Hochhuth was sued not long ago—along with his producer, Kenneth Tynan, and director, Clifford Williams—by a Czech ex-pilot who had been accused, in *Soldiers*, of helping to assassinate Sikorski on orders from Winston Churchill. All the defendants were forced to pay substantial damages.

I have been trying to sort out my feelings on this question. I share an instinctual American distaste for the prospect of legal restraints on freedom of expression; yet there is little doubt that people should have the right of protection against public pillory, whether in print, in the broadcast media, or on the documentary stage. The issue raises interesting problems for civil liberties, since in a case like this the liberty of the reporter is enjoyed only at the expense of the liberty of his subject, and the public gets its information at the cost of the individual's privacy. It is not just that some of these charges are sensational and irresponsible—civil libertarians often find themselves defending morally repugnant examples for the sake of a general principle—but rather that we are confronted here with a choice of two conflicting principles, each of them important.

I think the problem can be somewhat clarified if we consider the relationship of the media to ordinary citizens separately from the media's relationship to well-known personalities. England's libel laws are protective of, and sometimes overly sensitive to, the rights of private individuals because the country values privacy. Possibly because the country also believes in political accountability, these laws make little provision for protecting figures in the public eye. It is significant, for example, that Harold Wilson made no effort to retaliate against *Private Eye* for the aspersions cast on *his* sexual life, and that the Churchill family did not take to the courts to defend the reputation of its relative against the imputations in *Soldiers*. Vulnerability to slander has always been a companion to fame and power; and since history is usually made by powerful men, it is only just that history be allowed to vindicate their reputations. (In this regard, it is one of history's ironies that Conor Cruise O'Brien, whose *Murderous Angels* recently played here, is being vilified in Ireland, where he now holds public office, with much the same recklessness that, as a playwright, he once attacked Dag Hammarskjöld.)

The English freedom from official retaliation has been further extended with the recent lifting of the censorship laws. Now even the monarchy is exposed to theatrical scrutiny. The first fruit of this new freedom is an arthritic work called *Crown Matrimonial,* which has just appeared on the West End—an imaginary account of the family discussions at Marlborough House preceding the abdication of Edward VIII. Undistinguished in all other ways, this royal soap opera manages to send a little *frisson* through the audience with the appearance of an actress playing the present Queen Mother, chattering along with such animated Tussauds as Queen

Mary, the Duke of York, and the abdicating King. Standing vigil on the monarchy—this promises to become a continuing theatrical pastime now that *Crown Matrimonial* has broken the seals on the keyholes.

Still, this kind of thing remains pretty formal and respectful, probably because of the awe with which the royal family is still regarded in England. But even satire on political figures here (despite a little venom from the Fringe) never quite achieves the virulence that marked such American indictments as Barbara Garson's *MacBird,* Emile de Antonio's *Millhouse,* and Philip Roth's *Our Gang.* This may be because the English feel their public figures are less deserving of virulence; more likely, it stems from a certain vestigial hesitation about exposing privacies even in the lives of the most prominent public men.

I regard the freedom to satirize our Presidents as one of the most refreshing things about American culture, and one of our last defenses against an annihilating sense of political impotence. But it is difficult to deny that the openness of this criticism has become possible only in a society that has obliterated privacy and countenanced official spying. While the English accept some restrictions on free expression in order to protect the individual, we pay for our unbridled license by living in homes without doors or windows, where the media rampage through our living rooms and the Nixon administration through our telephone system. Cases are tried in the press before they even reach the courts; and the agonies of dying men, whether victims of war or the assassin's bullet, are invariably floodlit by a hundred popping flash bulbs. Those who express dissent against a criminal war policy are not publicly stifled; but they are sometimes hounded by investigative agencies and harassed in the courts with illegally accumulated evidence. A national administration is reinstated in office, with an overwhelming plurality, even though it has invaded the privacy of the opposition in a manner that would have brought down any government in Europe.

Meanwhile the nation sits drowsily before its television set, drinking down scandals with a bottle of beer. And although it prophesies the corruption of justice and the deterioration of the political process, the Watergate affair is absorbed as just another piece of entertainment on the evening news. American homes are opened to the television camera, the microphone, and the electronic bug; the Peeping Tom and the Eavesdropper displace the eagle on the mantelpiece. No wonder England puts some limits on the right to penetrate a citizen's sanctuary when the alternative is the media's glare, the government's secret surveillance.   (1972)

The Great American Tragedy

The Great American Disaster is the name of a small restaurant in the Chelsea district of London whose menu consists entirely of milk shakes and quarter-pound hamburgers. Patronized by overseas visitors and expatriates, it offers a decent approximation of American food to the indecent accompaniment of overamplified music—but more startling than its sound effects or bill of fare is its décor. The walls of this restaurant have been plastered with selected front pages of the *New York Times,* heralding through panic headlines the various catastrophes of the American century: the sinking of the *Titanic,* the Lindbergh kidnapping, the Depression, the two world wars, Little Rock, the Kennedy assassination. As for more recent events, these have been recorded in a brightly colored poster (which customers can buy for a pound) depicting the history of the past ten years in a montage of virulent caricatures.

These caricatures show, among other things, President Nixon ravening down a bloody piece of meat in the shape of Vietnam; Spiro Agnew in a playsuit, squatting in a nursery sucking on his foot; New York exploding in a cloud of poison, pills, and pollution; a vicious black panther leaping out of the mouth of an angry black man; a more cheerful black man sweeping garbage off the tongue of the Statue of Liberty; a bucolic landscape being chewed to bits by a mechanized monster belching smoke and filth; and a fat vacationer sweating under a burning Florida sun that bears the letters "U.S.A." —the "U." and the "A." being policemen with clubs beating up a Negro whose supine body forms the "S."

The poster is captioned "A Great Place for Hamburgers but Who'd Want to Live There," and its message embodies the kind of thing you might expect from a colony of exiles who leaven their nostalgia for an abandoned country with their reasons for leaving in the first place. Still, despite its bitter tone, the poster is not to be dismissed as mere expatriate bravado, for it encapsulates, in apocalyptic terms, many of the apprehensions that, in milder form, English people feel about America at the present time. So powerful are these anxieties among the English, in fact, that they don't even find expression in the usual anti-Americanism any more. A visitor to England in the past, even one highly critical of his own nation, usually found himself obliged to defend America against the force of English rancor and disdain. Now disdain has given way to concern, and just as a sick child is inquired after by a troubled relative, so America has become the subject of gentle questioning and quiet commiseration.

The extent of this solicitude can be measured by the growing preoccupation in the English media with American subjects. One is prepared for careful coverage of the recent elections, but it is surprising to find this interest extended into other aspects of our society. Alistair Cooke's affectionate and innocuous video history of America appears weekly here, as it does in the United States; and last night, all three channels of British television were dominated by American fare: an interview with Jimmy Stewart on BBC 1, a John Ford movie on BBC 2, and an episode from *The FBI* on ITV. The talk shows, moreover, are filled with conversations about American life. Arnold Beichman's book *Nine Lies About America* may very well have attracted more attention here than it did in its own country—probably because the title gave promise of a more positive view of Americans than English people usually hear these days. After being interviewed on BBC, however, and debated on ITV by another American (Ronald Dworkin, Professor of Jurisprudence at Oxford), Beichman proved incapable of sustaining even this slim hope. What he called "lies" often appeared to be little more than overstatements of obvious truths, and his bellicose efforts to justify American policies were gracefully parried by Dworkin's patient documentation and the English moderator's embarrassed remonstrances.

In the theatre, curiosity about America takes the form of a significant increase in productions of American plays. Our musicals, of course, have always been popular in the West End, and, like most of them, the recently opened *Applause* will undoubtedly survive its unenthusiastic notices. Our more highly touted serious plays are also imported regularly, though to a less certain fate—Paul Zindel's *The Effect of Gamma Rays on Man-in-the-Moon Marigolds,* for example, was coldly received here after an indifferent production at the Hampstead Theatre Club exposed all its clumsy plotting, old-fashioned naturalism, and unacknowledged debts to *The Glass Menagerie*.

Also exposed by this production was the extreme hardship English actors experience in trying to play American characters. (If you have any doubt of this, compare Paul Newman's superior movie version, which manages to disguise, through sensitive performances, all the inadequacies of Zindel's play.) It seems to be very difficult for English lips, long accustomed to trilled "r"s and long "a"s, to wrap themselves around American idiomatic speech—which proves the local witticism that England and America are two countries separated by a common tongue. How many English actors have been convincing in American parts? Peter Sellers in *Dr. Strangelove* is an obvious exception, playing a prissy President right out of the back rooms of American liberal politics; but Sellers is a brilliant impersonator rather than a skilled actor. And while Nicol Williamson scored a triumph recently on British TV playing Brecht's Arturo Ui in the manner of a brutal Mafia chieftain from Chicago, the accent was broad enough to be approached through mimicry.

The difficulty in performing our plays, as well as the growing interest in them here, is being further demonstrated at the National Theatre where two out of the four works in the fall

repertory are now American. Both of these—Hecht-Mac-
Arthur's *The Front Page* and Eugene O'Neill's *A Long Day's
Journey into Night*—are proving extremely popular with their
audiences; both have been directed by Michael Blakemore;
and both suffer in production from a similar failure to capture
the peculiar characteristics of the American experience.

The Front Page begins promisingly enough, when the
curtain opens to permit a cloud of tobacco smoke to pour into
the audience from the pressroom of the Chicago Criminal
Courts building (a setting brilliantly rendered by Michael
Annals). But it is soon clear from the laborious way in which
the action proceeds (the performance lasts almost three hours)
that the work is being treated in a curiously reverential way.
Entrances are prepared for in a manner more appropriate
to opera than to farce, and the wisecracks are delivered with
an italicized emphasis usually reserved for epigrams. The
rhythm turns legato, a vacuum of energy develops center
stage, and in place of the rattling dialogue and frenetic action
that are the strengths of the play, we get an undue stress on
its weaknesses of plot and character. Denis Quilley has a
certain racy gusto as Hildy Johnson that reminds me of Robert
Preston; but it isn't until late in the play, with the entrance of
Alan McNaughtan as Walter Burns, that any spikes begin to
break through the general lethargy.

If the National's version of *The Front Page* lacks the requisite
energy, its rendering of *A Long Day's Journey* lacks the
necessary pain and passion—a greater shame because the
production fails a greater play. One can understand how
English actors might confuse an Irish-American family with a
family in Ireland, and introduce a hint of brogue in place of a
New England accent. But while the unconvincing dialects are
annoying, what is most disappointing is the inability of the
cast to penetrate the suffering of these benighted characters.
The relationships of the four Tyrones should be as nagging as
a toothache; but what we get instead of painful accusations
and apologies is a beautifully spoken, rather polite series of
conversations among reserved and well-mannered house-
holders.

Playing Jamie and Edmund, Denis Quilley and Ronald

Pickup, though two excellent actors, failed to investigate the confessional poetry of their parts or their mutual interaction on each other; and while Constance Cummings, as Mary Tyrone, seemed to be moving toward something extraordinary in the terrain of her particular hell, she hit a detour somewhere in the third act and couldn't recover direction in time for her final speech. As for Sir Laurence Olivier—one of the finest actors in the world playing one of the world's greatest roles—he attacked the elder Tyrone like a character in classical comedy, speaking his lines as if they were verse, and displaying ease only with the miserly side of the character. One had to remember back to the great performance of Frederic March in the original production—self-justifying, raging, mixing reproaches with conciliation and compassion with despair—to recall the torment out of which this part and, indeed, this whole play were initially conceived.

What one missed most from the English production, finally, were the pity and the terror of the work—the sense of journey into an awful, almost unacknowledgeable past where hope is blighted by memory. The generic word for this is tragedy. And I am beginning to conclude, on the basis of more evidence than the inadequacies of this production, that tragedy is not a very congenial expression of the English theatre at the present time, even at the highest level of performance. Perhaps the English are paying a price for their extraordinary civic organization in that the security provided by public order is dulling the nation to the resources of the inner life. To be sure, there is a tragic skeleton in the British closet called Ireland— and the younger dramatists are now trying to rouse some shame and indignation over England's part in the past and present difficulties of Ulster. But perhaps because Ireland is separated from England by a sea's breadth, nobody here seems sufficiently upset by these accusations to enter into guilty explorations of the self.

America, on the other hand, is now in agony as a result of its past, and the afflictions of our nation are directly traceable to the errors and crimes of our history. As a result, I believe, we are becoming, perhaps without quite knowing it yet, a truly tragic nation. Our tragedy is a compound of

Vietnam, of deteriorating cities, of poverty and suffering and racial strife, of drug abuse and violence, of political assassination—and, further back, a heritage of the original sin of our country, the institution of slavery. A people who till very recently smiled at itself daily in the mirror, accentuated the positive, and demanded happy endings to its plays and movies is now being forced, against its will, to examine its soul and live with the knowledge that past sins are not easily redeemable, even with the best intentions.

This is the knowledge that forms the basis for the tragic art. It is small comfort, to be sure, to say that our present agonies are giving us a tragic dimension, for tragedy, being purgative rather than remedial, has never been known to solve a social problem or answer a political question. Still, if we can develop the courage to create and absorb tragedy in art, we may yet achieve the tough-mindedness we need to grapple effectively with the more insoluble difficulties of our society. And anyway, great art has always been a spiritual satisfaction rather than a utilitarian instrument—one of the few consolations left us in a bad, yes, a disastrous time. (1972)

Repertory in the Doldrums

The taproot of the English theatre since the war, unarguably, has been the repertory movement outside of London. Not only fertile in itself but the cause of fertility in others, this movement has nurtured artists for the RSC and the National Theatre, channeled plays and productions into the West End, and (as I can attest from experience with an American company) profoundly influenced the shape and substance of theatres throughout the world. Still, for all its apparent health and vigor—despite the steady growth of community support and new physical plants—the English repertory movement seems, in some areas, to have become momentarily stalled.

I suspect this may be a consequence of its very success,

since stability has a tendency to make you rest with easy answers when you ought to be asking yourself difficult questions. For example, is the repertory goal to be reached by choosing the safe and routine or by testing untried formulas? Should the repertoire of a provincial theatre be essentially regional—local plays about local problems—or should it include more general themes and universal considerations? Is it a theatre's obligation to turn out anthology plays in textbook productions, or should it be commissioning new works, unearthing neglected works of the past, and exploring contemporary avenues into the familiar masterpieces? To whom does the theatre owe its primary allegiance: to the audience, to the actors, to the playwright—or to some overarching idea that hovers over them all?

In the course of recent travels, I have had the opportunity to watch a number of provincial companies in the process of trying to answer these questions—seldom in satisfactory ways. At the Oxford Playhouse, for example, the company mounted a production of Molière's *The Misanthrope* in which there was so little effort at characterization that the cast was virtually indistinguishable. Translated into leaden academic verse, placed inside a characterless perspective setting, and performed by windup toys producing artificial gestures and verbal rattle, the production had the look of an institutional artifact rather than a spontaneous work of art, with the director-translator functioning as curator. As so often happens with such attempts at historical reconstruction, only the surface of the play was rendered while its most interesting feature—Molière's ambivalence toward Alceste's antisocial misanthropy—was left totally undramatized. I didn't stay to see it through, partly because I felt rising in me some of Alceste's rage against inauthentic art.

I was attracted next to Nottingham by a rare opportunity to see Ibsen's *Brand*, a brilliant but inordinately difficult work that few companies have had the temerity to produce. A few minutes after the curtain rose in Nottingham's comfortable playhouse, it was clear that not courage but foolhardiness was animating this event, since the company bashed through the play insensible that it possessed any difficulties at all. The set was one of those arrangements of Stonehenge dolmens on a turntable, lighted so amateurishly that the papier-mâché surface was clearly discernible.

Still, the set was visible, which is more than could be said for the actors. Although Brand is motivated by a passion to find the light, the lighting designer was curiously reluctant to oblige him, with the result that the actor was forced to look for God and the baby pink at the same time. This Brand was really benighted, and a little benumbed as well, surrounded as he was by a chorus of townspeople who spoke all their lines in unison. (Brand's delivery was so monotonous that he seemed to be speaking in unison, too.) I gather that both the director and the chief actor had previously performed the play on radio; I am reminded of the observation that the best thing about radio is the scenery.

After trials of this sort, it was with eagerness that I returned to a scene of previous pleasure to see the Actors' Company production of Iris Murdoch's *The Three Arrows* at the Cambridge Arts Theatre. This company—already responsible for an inspired version of *'Tis Pity She's a Whore*—is a close-knit ensemble of gifted actors, organized for the purpose of choosing their own plays, their own directors, and their own membership. There are obvious advantages to this democratic scheme; the obvious disadvantage is that plays will be selected less for intrinsic merit than for roles.

Miss Murdoch's play is not exactly an actor's vehicle, but if it weren't for its juicy parts, I doubt that it would have found its way into the company's repertoire. Set in medieval Japan, and written in a lapidary style half composed of modern colloquialisms and half of haiku epigrams, the play concerns a revolutionary prince, imprisoned for five years by imperial enemies, who gets the opportunity for release from prison through marriage with the emperor's sister. He must first choose among three arrows, representing the political, the religious, and the romantic life—the right choice brings him the princess, the wrong one his death. His enemies arrange that he fail the ordeal, but at the last moment the emperor intervenes, offering him the option of freedom without the princess. This he accepts; the lady kills herself; and after a little more carnage the prisoner sadly escapes.

This fable has some charm, but it is slight. And although Miss Murdoch contrives to pad out the evening with considerable wit, Zen philosophy, sword fights, and comedy scenes, there is something linear and scenically abrupt about the play's construction, something lacking in true inevitability that tempts one to nod. Noël Willman has directed the work efficiently, in a manner influenced partly by Kurosawa, partly by Gilbert and Sullivan, and the company, as expected, provides performances of singular delicacy and strength, but then this company would look good performing the London street guide.

Still, fine acting is a means, not an end; something more is needed to rescue the repertory movement from the doldrums. What I am still seeking is a theatre willing to risk its existence in order to advance its frontiers, continually questioning its direction even at the loss of its comfort and security. In a period when poetry, intelligence, and imagination are in such short supply, the theatre must have a higher purpose than the production of staples, for the famished spirit cannot be satisfied with the mere consumption of victuals, even when cooked to a turn and garnished with delights. I say this with full knowledge of all the persuasive economic arguments why the community must be satisfied and the audience left belching; and I am not romantic enough to believe (as some Fringe groups presumably do) that mere experimentation is equivalent to meaningful art. But I can't shake off the feeling that the repertory movement may be failing a marvelous opportunity for theatrical growth and renewal—an opportunity that won't present itself as long as theatres are trading their birthrights for a mess of bricks and mortar. (1972)

The Curses of Caliban
Kaspar

Rather than review Peter Handke's *Kaspar* (Almost Free Theatre) as a play, I am tempted to examine it as an argument, since, for all its absurdist devices, the work takes the form of a philosophical demonstration, based on hypotheses with which I cannot entirely agree. The fundamental assumption behind *Kaspar* is that language represents a brutalizing instrument of repression that is employed by society—through such agents as parents, teachers, journalists, and bureaucrats—to transform the free unconditioned individual into a subservient puppet of the state. I realize that this hostile view of language is rather current these days in the theatre, as well as in some philosophical circles; Peter Brook, for example, has apparently become so inhibited by the restrictions of coherent speech that he has recently been conducting experiments with an invented tongue called Orghast (and Brook produced *Kaspar*, I am told, as a preparatory exercise for his Paris group). But while language, admittedly, can be used for totalitarian purposes, and for the fabrication of social lies and aesthetic disasters, it can also be the occasion for extraordinary liberation. It is true that society exacts a price from human beings in return for speech and ordered thoughts; it is also true that the conceptual satisfactions of clear prose and the metaphorical splendors of fine poetry are among the major consolations for living with the discontents of civilization.

If I were happier with the theme of *Kaspar*, I might be less dissatisfied with its repetitive form, but the play strikes me as somewhat cumbersome and unwieldy. I am full of respect for Handke's seriousness, and am willing to concede that some of the play's limitations can be traced to his uncompromising reach. *Kaspar* is the work of a young man, but one with undeniable gifts; in fact, compared with most of the pretentious and imitative efforts of the post-Beckett avant-garde, it has real integrity, even considerable originality. Still, the mere mention of Beckett's name is enough to suggest how much more economically *Kaspar* might have been written, and with how much less glumness and irritability. (Actually, Beckett already did much the same thing, very simply, in the Lucky-Pozzo scenes of *Waiting for Godot*.) It is a tribute to Beckett's artistry that one can disagree with his metaphysics while responding to his plays; I am not sure the same can yet be said of Handke.

But to the play . . . *Kaspar* was partially inspired by the story of Kaspar Hauser, who, having spent the first seventeen years of his life in a closet, first communicated with the outside world through a single sentence: "I want to be someone like somebody else once was." The same sentence is repeated endlessly by Handke's Kaspar—the primitive demand for social identity that begins his social conditioning. As a group of cool, anonymous speakers bombard him with instructions, model sentences, clichés, syllogisms, proverbialisms—their voices sometimes tortured by overloaded loudspeakers and squealing electronics—Kaspar develops from a wild, disordered creature, mewling at inanimate objects and pulling furniture apart, into a neat, well-regulated, domesticated, and rather lobotomized member of society. In short, the play is a Romantic's view of history and phylogeny, encapsulating the progress of the child into adulthood, the ignorant into learning, the savage into civilization, the lunatic into sanity—always at the cost of considerable shame and agony.

During most of this unsentimental education, Kaspar is joined by four other Kaspars, who mock his growing awareness with their idiot antics—grappling with boxes, rattling paper, filing away at him with emery boards. Such imbecility reduces all Kaspar's achievements to zero; what he finally perceives is Othello's chaos of goats and monkeys. He has traded his inarticulacy for another form of imprisonment: "I have been made to speak. I have been sentenced to reality." By the end, Kaspar no longer wants to be somebody else; he only wants quiet. But the end of his isolation has doomed him to noisy desperation, and he is left without even the energy of protest. The play lacks quiet also, though it embodies plenty of protest, the author's remorseless grinding of the audience reminding one of Caliban's snarl at Prospero: "You taught me language; and my profit on't is, I know how to curse."

Robert Walker's production, a plausible confrontation with the play, takes place within a striking setting by Gabriella Falk, consisting of brightly painted furniture and colored pastel squares that give the impression of an antiseptic play-room. Henry Woolf plays Kaspar with a large degree of impishness, trailing his long shoelaces along the floor, pounding the walls in frustration, beetling his dark brows; and it is more a criticism of the play than of his performance to say that the part would have seemed less boring played by a great clown (say, Zero Mostel). Still, if *Kaspar* is something less than a new avant-garde landmark, it is an unusual play, significant not so much for what it is as for what it promises— sometimes penetrating, sometimes brilliant, always permeated by a fierce, if rather cold, intensity. (1973)

Mr. Arden Versus Mr. Jones

Until a short time ago, the only scandal in the English theatre was its paucity of interesting plays, but now a scandal of major proportions has broken out over the production of John Arden's *The Island of the Mighty*, at the Aldwych, by the Royal Shakespeare Company. Originally conceived in 1966 as a trilogy for television about the historical King Arthur, then canceled by the BBC for lack of funds, the work was later rewritten for the National Theatre of Wales to com-memorate its opening. When *The Island of the Mighty* proved too vast for the resources of the projected Welsh theatre as well, the RSC agreed to produce the play in a shortened version, and Mr. Arden proceeded to cut it down to four hours, meanwhile reworking the material in collaboration with his wife, Margaretta D'Arcy.

Relations between Arden and his director, David Jones, seemed perfectly amicable during the six-week rehearsal period—until Miss D'Arcy arrived from Ireland to witness the first full run-through, and promptly denounced the music, the acting, the setting, and the interpretation. According to Mr. Jones, Miss D'Arcy demanded radical changes, particularly in the songs and physical production, and when Mr. Jones refused—citing the rapidly approaching opening date and emphasizing that Mr. Arden had already approved of all the elements she disliked—the two authors decided to withdraw from the production, demanding an immediate company meeting at which to explain their stand. Jones denied this request, pleading scheduling problems, and he was supported in his decision by a large majority of the actors. As a result, the Ardens went out on strike as members of the Irish Society of Playwrights, setting up a two-person picket line outside the stage door of the Aldwych where they were photographed carrying such placards as "Playwrights Are Workers Before They Are Artists! Organize British Playwrights' Trade Union Now!"

Although a couple of the more jaundiced theatre critics suspected that the Ardens were throwing up a political smoke screen to hide an artistic disaster, the playwrights insisted that their motivation was entirely ideological. In a release to the press, they protested that the RSC was staging "an anti-imperialist play so that it glorifies imperialism," adding that this was only to be expected from a theatre subsidized by a Tory government to "cultivate bourgeois society on a consumer level." The Ardens further noted that Jones's refusal to acknowledge their demands was a form of artistic imperialism where the director tyrannized over his collaborators in exactly the way that managerial capitalists exploited their workers. Finally, they advised the British public to skip *The Island of the Mighty* and go instead to a Fringe production of *The Ballygombeen Bequest*—their previous play about the swindling of an Irish tenant farmer by a greedy absentee

English landlord—but this advice proved difficult to follow, since *The Ballygombeen Bequest* was soon taken off as a result of a libel action against its authors.

Stung by charges that identified them with imperialistic dictators and labor exploiters, David Jones and Trevor Nunn (the artistic director of the RSC) released their own statement in the form of a letter to the London *Times,* which they posted on the wall of the theatre's buffet lounge side by side with a reproduction of the Ardens' letter. In this, they denied all accusations, repeated that Arden had been perfectly happy with the production until he came under the influence of his wife, and declared proudly that the RSC is a "basically left-wing organization" that has produced such ideologically acceptable playwrights as David Mercer, Mrozek, Gorky, Brecht, and Günter Grass. (Nobody has yet called the RSC to account for its association with such political infidels as T. S. Eliot, Harold Pinter, and William Shakespeare.) Interviews, broadsides, and manifestoes followed from both camps, Arden insisting that "the artist is a worker linked with other workers (i.e., actors) who must together demand rights from management," and Jones trying to express both his sense of innocence and his pain at seeing "someone whom I regard as one of Europe's leading dramatists sitting outside our stage door in the rain."

The affair reached its climax, according to Jones's account, when an actor from another theatre interrupted the play during a review by mounting the stage with a placard and demanding that the performance stop. At this point, the Ardens jumped on the stage as well, and Miss D'Arcy began to tear the scenery apart, after first having landed a well-aimed kick at the anatomy of Mr. Jones. Arden then tried to address the audience, but despite Jones's appeal to let him speak, the audience preferred to see the performance. "Look, are you actually saying to me that you wish me to leave this theatre?" asked the astonished Arden. "Yes!" roared the audience in a single voice. "In that case," replied Arden, "I will leave this theatre and never write one word for you again."

Arden's promised silence as a writer apparently did not

extend to his new career as a striking protester, since he went directly from the theatre to take up his position outside the stage door, where he was joined by a few sympathizers, including the intrepid Joan Littlewood. (At that very moment, as we were later to learn from still another letter to the *Times,* Miss Littlewood was being unsuccessfully paged at her own theatre to answer a call from an outraged playwright protesting that she had treated his play in the same high-handed fashion that Jones reputedly treated the Ardens'!) And there, for all I know, Arden now stands with his wife, rain-soaked and bedraggled, the first playwright in history to picket his own play.

All this is so delicious that it has obscured all other theatrical events here. And no wonder. There is more insight into human folly in this absurd episode than in the entire London season so far, and more drama in Miss D'Arcy's kick than in all four hours of *The Island of the Mighty.* I find myself unable to arbitrate this dispute, since the production is everything the Ardens say it is: the songs are monotonous and urban, the settings romantic, the acting is gruff and colorless, the direction is lumbering. On the other hand, since the play is overwritten, pretentious, and waterlogged, it may be just the production that the Ardens deserve. As for all this talk about imperialism and anti-imperialism, it leaves me baffled. Mr. Arden expatiates in his program notes about the Third World and how the early history of Britain foreshadows twentieth-century turbulence, but aside from some conversation in the opening scene about the North Sea herring trade, the play contains as much political or economic significance as a high-school pageant, which it often resembles.

The Ardens have used *The Matter of Britain* (a scattering of writings about the historical Arthur) as a basis for an episodic spectacle about the Romanized Celts, the savage Picts, and the blond invaders from the Germanic countries called the English. For the customary chivalry and romance associated with Camelot, they have substituted a mélange of alliances, battles, tactics, stratagems, rapes, and murders, done to the accompaniment of primitive rituals and mythic

noises. None of the characters is permitted a personal revela-
tion, and even a brief intrigue between Guinevere and
Mordred serves only as a pretext for a realignment of forces,
perhaps on the mistaken notion that Brechtian drama is entirely public, and that nothing recognizably human should be
allowed to penetrate theatricalized history.

Although the English theatre is suffering such agonies for
the first time, this kind of controversy should sound pretty
familiar to Americans, since it closely parallels a number of
our own more celebrated broils, most notably that between Jules
Irving and Ed Bullins over the staging of *The Duplex* at the
Forum. Mr. Bullins, you will remember, complained bitterly
in the press about the Lincoln Center production of his play,
though, like Mr. Arden, he had already approved of the
director and the actors. (Bullins's complaints, coincidentally,
also seem to have centered on the music.) Like the Ardens, he
found a political reason for the putative mishandling of his
play, in this case calling the theatre not an imperialist agency
but rather a white establishment institution. Like the Ardens
again, Mr. Bullins tried to disrupt a performance of his play,
in company with a number of sympathizers. And finally, like
David Jones, Jules Irving discovered himself on stage pulling
out his liberal credentials in an effort to defend himself
against charges of racism, Fascism, dictatorship, and all the
other loose epithets of our embattled and reckless time.

There are lessons to be learned from all of this, though it
is doubtful if anyone will heed them. The first is that no art
of consequence will ever emerge out of a politicized atmosphere where the unspoken contract of civility gives way to
bad-tempered union hassles, and where, in place of a creative
collaboration presided over by one person who makes decisions, a form of democratic anarchy prevails. The second is
that liberal theatre directors, perhaps because they are uneasy with authority, tend to become perfect patsies for contro-
versialists who can easily bend them into contortions of
tolerance, benevolence, and apology. The last is that radical
playwrights—after first deciding that they want their plays
produced in the most lavish circumstances, with a minimum
of problems and (though it is cruel to say it) a maximum of

publicity—are frequently obliged later to start a ruckus in order to persuade themselves and their admirers that they have not capitulated to the enemy.

What, then, have the Ardens proved by this media tempest? That subsidized theatres are imperialist? No, merely that it is easy to make their liberal directorship feel guilty. That playwrights are workers before they are artists? No, rather that they cease to be artists when they pretend to be workers. That (as a character says in *The Island of the Mighty*) "the poets alone can prevent catastrophe"? No, only that poets can contrive better reasons to justify their violent actions than more prosaic mortals. Most of all, they have proved that good theatres begin to decline when they choose plays for political rather than artistic reasons; and that writers who claim both the rewards of the system and the purity of a radical conscience end up not overthrowing society but merely providing it with another source of entertainment. (1973)

The Evolution of a Woman
A Doll's House

Ibsen's *A Doll's House* is presently being performed at the Criterion with considerable clarity and power in one of those rare productions that manage to expand your understanding of familiar material without resorting to unfamiliar metaphors. Of all Ibsen's plays, this is the most difficult to revive, being the most well-worn; but under Patrick Garland's fastidious direction, aided by an eloquent adaptation from Christopher Hampton and by John Bury's and Beatrice Dawson's handsome setting and costumes, *A Doll's House* comes through with all the vitality and surprise of a brand-new work. Inevitably, partisans of the women's movement have claimed the play for their cause, and there is little question that Ibsen is partly investigating here the subjugation of women by men.

What is remarkable about the play, however, is not its "relevance" to contemporary issues, since this would soon make its theme as stale and flat as its relatively clumsy stage mechanics. No, the play is interesting rather as a study of a human being in the process of awakening from self-deception and false social values; and it is this more universal side of Nora that Claire Bloom explores in her pensive and persuasive performance.

Ibsen has saddled the actress playing Nora with an almost impossible dilemma, which Miss Bloom solves admirably: how to make an immediate transition, on the basis of a single discovery, from dependent child bride to determined, resourceful, and independent woman. Miss Bloom prepares for her final scene from the beginning of the play by demonstrating how Nora's early stratagems and deceptions are the circuitous form of a thwarted intelligence, and her flirtatiousness a substitute for straightforward expressions of will. In her early moments, she shows us Nora leaping up and down while touching her fingers to her nose like a squirrel, and (in a gesture which should make every man in the audience feel ashamed) begging money from Torvald's hand like a puppy going for biscuits. But underneath the flighty mannerisms exists a woman of considerable shrewdness and perspicacity who can manipulate Dr. Rank with subtle sexuality (the flesh-colored stockings scene somehow becomes more voluptuous here than the most flagrant erotic display), while making the stage vibrate, when her secret is about to be exposed, with fiercely controlled hysteria. Nora's slamming of the door thus becomes a terrifying act of moral courage, performed by a woman who has determined to stop playacting and express her native qualities of character in much less circular ways.

This is a major performance for which the rest of the cast provides relatively strong support. Anton Rogers meliorates Rank's gloom with irony and humor, and Stephanie Bidmead's Mrs. Linde manages to be tough and realistic without losing her compassionate humanity. Unfortunately, Peter Woodthorpe plays the reluctant blackmailer, Krogstad, like a Dickens villain, and sometimes like a creature from Hammer films—bulging his eyes and curling his lip, as if he were about to suck on the nearest available artery. As for Colin Blakeley, he manages to make the stolid, patronizing stick-figure Torvald into something relatively complicated—and occasionally quite amusing, too, in his smug self-satisfaction—but he loses emotional energy at the crucial moment of discovery, and collapses into whining falseness when Nora most requires a convincing antagonist. The performance, in short, is persuasive only as long as it rests on technique; when it needs to draw on feeling as well, it develops a certain hollowness in contrast with the passionate truthfulness of Miss Bloom.

It is, in fact, Miss Bloom's sense of truth, along with her personal beauty and intelligence, that rescues this play from the tractarian grip of issues and movements. Some actresses will undoubtedly play the final scene as if they were slamming the door on Torvald's genitals; Miss Bloom's Nora closes it on her own delusions. She has abandoned husband, home, and children not as an act of disgust or hostility but in order to discover her self, because she cannot possibly be qualified as a wife and mother until she has learned how to be a human being. The indictment of society is all the more terrible for being implicit, while the alternative to its rigid social codes is not some narcissistic form of "liberation," but rather a rediscovery of the relationship between obligations to others and obligations to one's self. Preserving her civility, accepting her loneliness, expanding her humanity, Ibsen's Nora shows us the true meaning of independence, as well as the cost it exacts in sacrifice and isolation; in short, she shows us that freedom and responsibility are virtually inseparable. I am grateful to this production for increasing my respect for this play. (1973)

Sam Shepard's America
The Unseen Hand

Sam Shepard's *The Unseen Hand* (Theatre Upstairs) was written in 1969, soon after the appearance of *Operation Sidewinder,* and, like that other excursion into the Western nightmare, it shows us an America in which myth and reality have become one. The setting is a shoulder of a California Freeway. There a 1956 Chevrolet Bel Air squats, stripped and derelict, surrounded by the flotsam of the American highway: bones, sawdust, used tires, empty cans of Budweiser beer. On an adjacent billboard, a smiling cartoon cowboy welcomes visitors to Azusa ("Everything from A to Z in the USA")—an actual town a few miles outside of Los Angeles whose name derives from the same slogan—and the playwright's imagination has obviously been dazzled by the kind of country that could invent such a place. *The Unseen Hand* is a hallucination based on fact—a compound of nostalgia and celebration in the face of the more tawdry elements of American life—which draws its energy from a compost heap, the flamboyant vulgarity of California culture.

Partly observed, partly absorbed, the characters of the play are a weird blending of authentic types and media constructs, as seen in McDonald's hamburger joints, bowling alleys, high-school stadiums, or in sci-fi movies, horror films, and Westerns. Taken together, they mingle past, present, and future into a pastiche of legend and actuality that describes prole America more effectively than the most fastidious documentary. Included in this bizarre gallery are: Blue Morphan, a 120-year-old juicer who makes his home in the back seat of the Chevy; the two brothers, brought back from the dead, with whom he used to hold up trains—Cisco, a scruffy desperado in a poncho, and Sycamore, a sinister figure in black, with a six-gun more than a foot long; the Kid, a brainless high-school cheerleader; and Willie, an eerie creature from a distant planet called Nogoland, who has been possessed by an unseen hand that squeezes his brain whenever he tries to "think beyond a certain circumference."

Shepard's approach is simply to place these disparate characters against a contemporary landscape and let them work upon each other: Willie subjects Blue to an electronic transformation that brings him back to the age of thirty; the Kid (his trousers are down throughout the play) has been whipped by supporters of the opposing team, who also tried to paint his balls black; the resurrected train robbers discover, to their grief, that they have lost their function because "there ain't no trains no more, just planes and Hovercrafts."

Shepard also throws in a plot of sorts, concerning the efforts of Willie to escape from the Hand, and to free his enslaved people from the Silent Ones. When the Kid tries to shoot him, screaming his love for Azusa to the accompaniment of a rock chorus ("I love the Junior Chamber of Commerce and the Kiwanis and the Safari Shopping Center and the Freeway and the Bank of America and the Donut Shoppes and the miniature golf course and setting off cherry bombs and my mom. . . ."), Willie breaks the spell of his intergalactic oppressor by reciting the Kid's litany backward, a language that turns out to be the ancient tongue of the Nogo. He returns to his planet, leaving the earth people stranded on theirs—reconciled to America, but afflicted with their own kind of brain possession.

Jim Sharman's production is splendid, a triumph for the Fringe, and his actors have located precisely the right identities for their characters: Warren Clarke's Blue Morphan, a salty derelict out of *The Treasure of the Sierra Madre;* Richard O'Brien's Willie, looking like Julian Beck and sounding like Peter Lorre, a fugitive from Mad Doctor movies; Christopher Malcolm as Sycamore, a hybrid of Wyatt Earp and Fearless Fosdick; and Clive Endersby, a bouncy Kid from the world of Andy Hardy. Fifties rock-n'-roll provides a whiff of pop nostalgia and the flag-draped Chevy is a striking piece of junk sculpture, while Neil Hansford's prepared piano plunks out a variety of melodies and sound effects. As for Shepard, he continues to confront American popular culture with a kind of manic exuberance—not exalting its every wart and pimple, like Andy Warhol, but nevertheless considerably turned on, like many of his generation, even by its more brutalized expressions. In a degenerate time, this may be a strategy for survival, and it certainly sparks the energy of *The Unseen Hand;* but I miss that quality of aloofness that would make this play not only a creative act but an act of moral resistance as well. (1973)

Acting in England and America

Whatever my various grumbles about the conventionality of the English theatre recently, its professional competence lies beyond dispute. There is something dependable about production here, even in the most predictable plays, which assures the spectator that few evenings in the theatre will ever be entirely wasted. It goes without saying that no such confidence exists in the United States. There even the most adventurous programs are too often hobbled by awkward performing or ham-handed directing, especially if the material wanders too far from the personal experience of the actors. The American theatre has made substantial achievements, but for several reasons a consistently high level of performance now seems to be the exception rather than the rule. Certainly we have good actors enough; still, our players are frequently unable to sustain their talents from one play to the next, or even during a consecutive run of the same production.

I've been considering lately why this should be so, and why —in spite of the recent development of acting programs designed to improve the situation—some of our training procedures may have exacerbated the problem rather than solved it. I suspect that the reasons may be not only aesthetic and technical but moral and social as well; indeed, our present dilemma probably arises from the very nature of the American temperament, if not from the quality of American life.

To speak in general terms, English society is stable, social-minded, concerned with the welfare of others, while American society is fragmented, anarchic, and obsessively involved with the problems of self. Reflecting this interest in the Other, the English actor approaches his role as if it were a mask (Olivier, for example, professes to discover the key to his part the moment he finds the right nose), varying his speech, gait, and features to suit the needs of the character. Reflecting his interest in the Self, the American actor usually purveys a single character from role to role, one that is recognizably close to his own personality. This subjective, autobiographical approach to performance is reflected in the most prominent American acting method where the current jargon includes expressions like "personalization" and "private moment," signifying techniques with which to investigate one's own psychic history.

The Actors Studio, which devised these techniques in the fifties through a mistaken reading of Stanislavski, was responsible for developing not character actors, willing to submerge themselves in the life of another, but rather personalities (many of them movie and TV stars) who often exploited their own personal quirks. The fiasco, at the 1965 World Theatre Festival, of the Actors Studio production of *The Three Sisters* was partly caused by the failure of its generally gifted performers to fuse themselves into a unified ensemble, but mostly by their inability to subordinate personal mannerisms to the requirements of Chekhov's characters. This problem proved fatal not only to the reputation of the Studio but to that of our theatre as a whole; apart from the Negro Ensemble, no American company has been invited to this prestigious festival since.

Nor did the various innovations of the sixties help much to objectify American acting. Performing ensembles such as the Living Theatre and its numerous offspring were simply an inevitable extension of a similar Romantic self-involvement. As Judith Malina once said, "I dig Shakespeare sometimes, but I want to speak in my own voice. I mean there's Hedda

Gabler, and there's Judith Malina, and I want to be Judith Malina." In short, such actors were refusing to perform unless they could appear in their own characters and speak their own lines; and it was not surprising, considering their questionable command of the language, that much of this work became physical rather than verbal.

There are, of course, a number of permanent companies scattered around the United States that perform classical and modern texts; and a few acting schools have tried to train their students for work in such theatres. But young people arriving at these schools often bring with them a native baggage of inarticulacy and self-absorption; and the burden of every acting teacher is to encourage such students to overcome their shyness about speaking out, to make them understand how to internalize the feelings of somebody else, and to help them to investigate the lives of others without rooting around too obsessively in their own. In short, while the histrionic impulse may be instinctual to many Americans, the mimetic or imitative impulse may not be; and acting programs have the insuperable task of trying to inculcate habits that are not naturally absorbed through the culture.

Obviously, such habits come naturally enough in England, where actors are able to appear before audiences without blushing or stammering, as relaxed on stage as in their own living rooms. (Some West End productions, indeed, sound like an extension of living-room conversation.) Cheerfully assuming the disciplines required to interpret a role intelligently, happily accepting a subordinate role in relation to a written text, the English actor is eager to offer the spectator everything he has—everything, that is, except the intimacies of his own life, about which he is as guarded as the American actor is exposed.

Generosity and effortlessness—these are the cardinal virtues of the English actor, and they arise from an informal, relaxed, and homogeneous relationship with the English spectator. The American actor, by contrast, often seems to be performing within an enclosed circle of constraint, with a great gulf dividing him from the indifferent witnesses in the house. Perhaps this separation is an inheritance of our traditional Puritan suspicion of the theatre; perhaps it is a sign that the American theatregoer, despite the huge amounts of money, time, and energy he spends to go to a play, really doesn't want to be there. Whatever the reason, much vital energy is exhausted by American actors in trying to bridge this gulf, either by enticing the audience to love them for their personal charms, like Broadway stars, or, like many performing groups, by trying to integrate the audience within the performance by means of special environments.

Both solutions strike me as artificial, and both signify that enterprises like the theatre can never be entirely without a healthy public and private life. In England, where the theatre evokes great pride as a national institution (Noël Coward's death, for example, was not only reported on the front pages of all the newspapers, but dominated radio and television for two days), the public services are marvelous and, as a result, privacy is respected, too. For it is a paradox that true privacy is possible only when the public life is blessed, because the existence of such congenial meeting places as the theatre and the pub gives the home a certain inviolability. You may not be invited often to English homes for dinner, but you won't find television cameras welcome there, either. The voluntary participation of the Louds in the televising of their disintegrating family life is simply inconceivable in England.

In the United States, on the other hand, where the public life is brutish and corrupt, the streets are unsafe, and the doors of the living room are open to the media, theatre is something created almost everywhere but on stage. The Actors Studio mystique of the "private moment," where actors are encouraged to expose whatever is most hidden and shameful in their lives, has now become a popular game among some well-known writers, personalities, and even ordinary citizens, as the country lolls about in an orgy of exhibitionism that makes every man an actor, and every man a spectator. Encounter groups, sensitivity sessions, feelies, and the whole desperate paraphernalia of contact are invented in the hope that physical proximity or public confession will somehow create links with strangers, while people divide along racial, sexual, and generational lines in a frantic search for brotherhood and community.

But somehow, for all their efforts to make everything public, Americans still remain lonely and isolated, which may explain why, though English audiences are still drawn to the theatre, American audiences are mostly drawn to the movies. The one is a private medium, dark and intimate, watched by the spectator in solitude; the other is a public medium, expressive and garrulous, enjoyed by the spectator in company with others. For this and other reasons, American actors gravitate toward the movies, too, our George C. Scotts and Paul Newmans remaining close to the cameras, despite brief periodic returns to the stage, while England's Paul Scofields and John Gielguds remain anchored to the stage, despite periodic appearances in movies. (This is inevitably reflected in the attitudes of the young. The American acting student asks, "How can I break into movies?" The English acting student asks, "How do I get into rep?") The exemplary theatrical career in England is that of Sir Laurence Olivier, who, after years in film, capped his career by presiding over the National Theatre; the most typical American development is that of Marlon Brando, who, after triumphing early in the stage version of *Streetcar*, went off to Hollywood where he has remained ever since, championing every cause except that of the stage, and doing a succession of often indistinguishable roles.

Yet Brando's recent performances in *The Godfather* and *Last Tango in Paris* suggest that for all its erraticism, clumsiness, and sheer waste of talent, American acting, at its best, somehow manages to penetrate more deeply than anything found on the English stage. And I would like to conclude this melancholy analysis by finding some hope in this rare occurrence. Theatre is said to be continually dying in America, and the difficulty of trying to keep it alive in barren soil is an anguish to which many (myself included) can testify. But the situation, while desperate, is not irremediable as long as careers like Brando's can be redeemed in such a powerful way. This admittedly remains a movie career; and there is a general feeling at the present moment, I gather, that it is becoming virtually impossible to form and to hold a permanent company of gifted stage actors. Nor can one minimize the difficulties of any cooperative enterprise in a society that honors only careerism and individual achievement.

Still, the very agonies that America is now suffering as a nation make it conceivable that theatrical breakthroughs may someday be achieved. The English have in their theatre an institution that enjoys vital health, but not much adventurousness. But we who suffer daily from the harrowing nature of our national life may, in the effort to find some pattern in our shards and fragments, create a theatre with the power to shake the soul. (For this, we have the example of O'Neill.) True, the possibilities are slim, and the odds are high; but if we can just make ourselves into a decent community, an American theatre may yet survive. (1973)

The Limits of English Realism

Any description of English theatre today would have to take notice of how firmly rooted it is in a tradition of social realism —by which I mean a preoccupation with the politics, morals, and manners of middle- or working-class life, treated with attention to surface authenticity. Now realism and its byproduct naturalism have constituted one of the mainstreams of modern drama since its beginning, moving from France to Scandinavia in the eighties and nineties, thence to Germany around the turn of the century, and dominating American plays from the twenties to the fifties, with particular ideological emphasis in the thirties. In England, however—if we discount the plays of Shaw (which owe as much to Gilbert and Sardou as to Ibsen or Brieux) and the fumbling efforts of Galsworthy, Pinero, and Henry Arthur Jones to develop a drama of social concern—true realism cannot be properly said to have reached these shores until the appearance of Osborne's *Look Back in Anger* in 1956.

That play created, virtually overnight, a radical change in the style of the British stage that was still apparent in 1965. After an extended visit to London during that year, I had occasion to write the following about what was then being called the New English drama: "The revolution that recently swept across the English stage succeeded in clearing away the debris of artificial drawing-room comedies, sterile well-made plays, and vacant pseudo-Elizabethan poetic dramas, but like the revolution in Depression America it created an ideological atmosphere in which many began to regard the drama as a weapon of class warfare. . . . The result is apparent in the new plays, many of which reek with sentimentality about the working class, excessive literalism, overinsistence on the grime and squalor of Midlands industrial cities, stale didacticism, and a kind of laziness about working out a theme in action."

At that time, I was writing primarily about such playwrights as Osborne, Wesker, Jellicoe, Waterhouse and Hall, Delaney, and Owen (Pinter and Arden were too idiosyncratic to be classified in any simple way); and eight years later (back for a longer look), I notice that the political didacticism I previously observed in their work has become rather muted, having passed to the group-authored plays of the Fringe, as well as to the now more polemical writings of John Arden. That point aside, however, little seems to have changed, except that my list of realistic playwrights would now be even longer, swelled to include all the theatrical Davids that aim their slingshots at Establishment Goliaths (David Storey, David Hare, David Mercer, David Halliwell), along with such writers as Peter Terson, Bill Bryden, Charles Wood, and E. A. Whitehead.

Now this is rather remarkable, considering that realism has largely lost its appeal for the most interesting postwar writers in the rest of the world, who usually ignore social-political themes and naturalistic techniques for experimental journeys into dream, metaphor, phantasmagoria. (The only other place, in fact, where realism dominates the stage today, outside of the Soviet Union, is in the American black theatre movement, which has remarkable similarities to the white Depression theatre of the thirties.) Beckett, Ionesco, and Genet in France; Handke in Germany, and Frisch and Dürrenmatt in Switzerland; Sam Shepard, Ronald Ribman, Jean-Claude van Itallie, and Robert Wilson in the United States—these are only a few representative Europeans and Americans who scorn verisimilitude, preferring interior poetry and metaphysical themes to a factual narrative based on realistic representation. By contrast, English playwrights—with the notable exceptions of Bond and Pinter (and, in a lighter vein, Stoppard)—are virtually unique in their continuing concern with class conflict, domestic relations, and social problems; and even Bond and Pinter occasionally use naturalistic conventions in formulating such plays as *Saved* and *The Homecoming*.

Why does realism continue to maintain its hold on the English stage long after it would seem to have exhausted its welcome most everywhere else? Partly, I would guess, because it developed so late here, partly because it is able to draw on such a rich fund of gifted actors. For the Osborne revolution not only inspired an entirely new mode of English playwriting in 1956, it was also responsible for a whole new approach to acting and directing, having recruited an army of lusty young men and women, often from working-class backgrounds, who were to invade the well-bred English stage, and transform it with their force and sardonic bite. Such was the power of performers like Albert Finney, Joan Plowright, Kenneth Haigh, Nicol Williamson, Ian Holm, Rita Tushingham, Frank Finlay, and others that playwrights soon began to write plays for them, with the result that actors were helping to perpetuate the very movement that had brought them into being.

One cannot fail to be struck by the extraordinary rapport between English writing and English acting, where the performer not only fulfills the requirements of his written role but also helps to supplement it with material from his own experience. Individual playwrights such as Chekhov and Brecht have occasionally been served like this before, but then only by companies especially trained for the purpose; and although Arthur Miller and Tennessee Williams profited in a similar way from their collaboration with members of the Actors Studio, the success of their plays on Broadway usually depended upon the participation of a single director, Elia Kazan.

So there are genuine advantages to the English system of realism, particularly in production. If the typical modern dramatist (Ibsen, Strindberg, Beckett) was often forced to write in isolation from a sympathetic company, the English playwright more often creates in the epicenter of a community, in collaboration with a host of like-minded actors, directors, and designers. On the other hand, there are certain disadvantages to this system for the writer, too, one of them being his sacrifice of an original point of view, if not of an independent style. Shakespeare wrote with actors like Kemp and Burbage in mind, but (though he was probably happy to revise his work to suit the actors' needs) it is doubtful if he willingly let them add their own interpolations to the verse that was already set down for them. For while actors are essential in bringing reality to a character, what is most real for them is not always most penetrating or eloquent for the play.

In short, while realism tends to make the actor comfortable, it also makes the playwright anonymous. A few English realists have managed to preserve an unmistakable voice, sometimes (like John Osborne) by turning away from realism altogether and ventriloquizing freely through the mouths of dramatic spokesmen. But more often, English realism is characterized by gray, exacting prose and halting dialogue, or the mistaken assumption that authenticity and inarticulacy are somehow inseparable.

This is not to say that realism cannot have its own poetry. A recent BBC play by Colin Welland called *Kisses at Fifty* provided tangible evidence (if any is needed after O'Casey, Odets, and Synge) that working-class speech can be idiomatically rich, racy, and flavorful. But such works as Bill Bryden's drama of Glasgow unionism, *Willie Rough,* and David Storey's portrait of Northern rugby league players, *The Changing Room,* are marked less by colloquial poetry than by relentless repetition and verbal fumbling, where every third word is "bloody" and virtually everybody speaks alike.

The Changing Room brings to mind another limitation of this kind of realism; its tendency to transform the audience into Peeping Toms. To avoid misunderstanding, I should declare immediately that I dislike audience-participation plays, and sympathize with Kenneth Tynan's impulse to apply a match to the bare feet of any actor foolish enough to climb over his lap. But the alternative to physical contact with actors is emotional and intellectual contact with plays—not a form of inert voyeurism where the spectator inspects documentary events with as much personal involvement as a laboratory technician examining microscopic particles. If the theatre does not draw you in, it remains nothing but a surface, however carefully ordered, and, however grim its subject, it cannot help but leave you placid and unmarked.

I say this out of full regard for all the meticulous care with which Mr. Storey has tried to authenticate his picture of players coming and going, removing and putting on their clothes, sustaining their injuries, and cutting up in the bathtub; and I respect the opportunity he offers actors—most recently the Long Wharf company at the Morosco—to give a persuasive impersonation of real-life football players behaving as they would in a real-life locker room. Quite obviously, I have failed to see all the mythic resonances and modern rituals that others have professed to find in the action, and should be glad to learn just how Mr. Storey's conscientious naturalism manages to transcend itself. But the result of all this pointless precision was to leave me, detached and slightly embarrassed, looking through the wrong end of a telescope at lives so special they eventually came to seem exotic.

And this finally is my beef about such realism in the theatre: that it lavishes so much time and expertise on creating effects that the documentary camera can achieve without the slightest effort. It is film that places the passive spectator before an unalterable surface, demanding his acquiescence as a witness to fixed, immutable events. But the theatre, which began as an act of religious involvement, is nothing without the elements of engagement and surprise. If the theatre is to survive in competition with its great technological counterpart, it will not be by throwing back a photographic reality at the spectator, but rather by generating perceptions and experiences that can only be created through living beings confronting other living beings in an imaginative act. Perhaps realism can still provide a springboard for the imagination—it has certainly done so in the past—but only if it breaks through the deception of surfaces to the perceptual reality beneath. (1973)

Thebes and Watergate

At the same time that the Watergate stench was rising in the United States, my wife, our child, and I were motoring through Greece, on our way to see the theatre at Delphi. In order to reach this breathtaking sanctuary along the Sacred Way from Athens, you must first drive through Thebes, past Mount Cithaeron, and over the Triple Way, a famous junction of roads near Delphi where, according to legend, Oedipus dragged Laius, his stranger-father, from his chariot and killed him after Laius had first struck him in the face with a whip.

All these places are mentioned in Sophocles' play, and it is remarkable how some familiarity with such locations enhances one's appreciation of Greek tragedy. (Aeschylus's *Agamemnon*, to cite another example, is much more comprehensible after a visit to the palace at Mycenae.) Yet, in some odd way, the breaking of the Watergate scandal at the time of the trip was just as helpful as geography in dramatizing the cogency of *Oedipus the King*, since it shares with the action of the play certain unmistakable parallels as well as several disturbing differences.

In Sophocles, Oedipus, at the peak of his fortune as head of state, learns that a crime-induced plague is polluting his city, and decides to cure it by determining the identity of the person responsible. ("Whoever he may be, whether he did the deed with others or by himself alone . . . it were a wrong to leave the guilt unpurged . . . and all have sinned that could have searched it out and did not.") Through remorseless investigation, he finally discovers that he himself is the source of the city's plague, having defiled Thebes by unwittingly killing his father and marrying his mother; and, acting as his own justicer, he stabs out his eyes and exiles himself from Thebes forever. Oedipus's character is his destiny. The very qualities that motivated his original deed—pride, honor, anger, impatience—are those that transform him into a tragic figure, one who both prosecutes and judges his own crime.

The comparisons with Watergate are obvious, if not odious. Richard Nixon, also at the peak of his fortune after a landslide victory unique in American electoral politics, is finally forced to concede that a plague of quite another sort is corrupting his country, and declares that he will cure it by bringing the criminals to justice. ("I want you to know beyond a shadow of a doubt that, during my term as President, justice will be pursued fairly, fully, and impartially no matter who is involved. . . . There can be no whitewash at the White House.") But instead of starting a thorough investigation, he does everything within his substantial power to obscure the truth— probably because, like Oedipus, he may himself be the defiler of the land. What he creates through such evasions as executive privilege, suppression of evidence, muzzling of witnesses is suspicion about himself, contempt for his office, and corruption in the very palace of justice, since his administration has used the investigative agencies of the nation not for exposing crime but rather for helping to commit it. Three millenniums after Oedipus, character is still destiny. The very qualities that motivated the original deed—ruthlessness, deceptiveness, power lust, contempt for the law—are those that characterize the later efforts to cover it up.

The contrast between the way King Oedipus and President Nixon behave in similar circumstances says much about the deterioration of statecraft and the disintegration of personal honor in American politics. But although the present story lacks a hero in high office, the truth has managed to emerge regardless; and the satisfaction one feels at this cannot be explained only as glee over Nixon's discomfiture. For me, the Watergate scandal is a striking confirmation of the assumptions of dramatic art, particularly the concept of poetic justice, for it proves (using the same compressed economy we find in the most powerful plays) that the qualities of man are ultimately decisive in ordering his fate. Oedipus, blind when he saw, plucked out his eyes as a judgment on his visionlessness. Nixon, whether he stays in office, resigns, is impeached, or banishes himself like Oedipus, will undoubtedly remain benighted, a prisoner of his character. Still, in this affair justice has regained its poetry, and what the Greeks called *hamartia* has once again functioned as an agency of the moral life. The ancient rubble of Greece, merely a pile of climbing rocks for my nine-year-old son, remains the embodiment of necessary myths—myths that operate still in our lives while rebuking the age with their power and example.   (1973)

In Defense of Repertory Theatre

For me, the most significant development in the English theatre this year has been the career of Diana Rigg. An attractive actress who first came to notice in America in a routine television series called *The Avengers,* Miss Rigg last year joined the National Theatre company, where she proceeded to play a variety of roles with ever-increasing command—among them, a neurotic rock singer in Tom Stoppard's *Jumpers,* a saturnine closet-witch Lady Macbeth in *Macbeth,* and, most triumphantly, a melancholy Célimène in the recent revival of Molière's *The Misanthrope.*

In Miss Rigg's interpretation of Célimène, this usually giddy coquette emerges as the most complicated character in the play, though the directorial approach has hardly been designed for depth. Performed in a witty, actable version by Tony Harrison that locates the action in a modern Paris presided over by Charles de Gaulle, John Dexter's production manages to circumvent the traditional English distaste for Molière by dressing him up to look like Wilde, Coward, or Stoppard—which is to say, a verbal acrobat in the English comedy-of-manners tradition. Molière's frivolous society of superficial courtiers is there all right—with Alceste behaving as superficially as everyone else. In the hands of that good actor Alec McCowen, Alceste is no longer a morose outsider, but rather a petulant and somewhat foppish sophisticate, as bitchy as the rest of Célimène's admirers, and equally unserious in his feelings toward her.

This is rather like playing Harpagon without his avarice or Tartuffe without his guile; but if McCowen's performance skirts the darker issues of the play, it is certainly compatible with the entertainment values of this glittering production—and it heightens unintentionally the more emotionally nuanced playing of Miss Rigg. The hostess of what seems to be an endless party, Miss Rigg's Célimène makes her first entrance in a barebacked dress to the strains of a bossa nova, and then —with a delicate blend of charm, chic, and sheer malice— proceeds to play fag-hag to the courtiers Acaste and Clitandre as they loll among her pillows, slaughtering reputations between shrieks of laughter and mouthfuls of champagne and caviar. Later, after she has been exposed, Miss Rigg adds a touch of chiaroscuro to the part, showing us a lonely but undefeated woman—onstage after everyone abandons her, gazing enigmatically at the evening lights of Paris.

Miss Rigg's progress as a repertory actress is significant to me because it reverses the usual history of theatre careers, particularly as pursued in America. Instead of being discovered on stage and then whisked off to Hollywood, Miss Rigg returned to investigate her talents as a classical performer *after* she had already established herself as a commercial star (she had actually begun her acting career in repertory); and although she will probably play in movies again, as well as in television, it is doubtful if she will ever stray for long from the kind of theatrical roles she now approaches with such strength and insight. Nor is hers an isolated development. The major stage performances in London this year have all been contributed by actresses who are already familiar from films: Billie Whitelaw in *Not I,* Janet Suzman in *Hello and Goodbye,* Maggie Smith in *Private Lives,* Eileen Atkins in *Suzanna Andler,* Claire Bloom in *A Doll's House.* That all these actresses were also originally repertory-trained may explain their intelligent choice of plays.

When American movie actresses make their infrequent appearances on stage, they usually star in Broadway musicals.

This reconfirmation of the repertory system in England comes at a time when its value is being seriously questioned in the United States; and it is in this larger context that the objections of its most vocal American critics ought to be examined. The stimulus for this criticism, by the way, was the collapse of the leadership of Jules Irving at the Repertory Theatre of Lincoln Center. Although this theatre was not a true repertory in the sense of rotating plays, it was the best-publicized example of a subsidized permanent company in the United States; and since Irving's was the third regime to fall at Lincoln Center in less than ten years, the failure inevitably aroused doubts about the future of permanent theatre as a whole—doubts that were increased when Joseph Papp, taking over the reins at the Beaumont, announced his intention to disband the company and produce on a project basis, as he now does at the New York Public Theatre.

Mr. Papp claims that repertory theatre at Lincoln Center is an idea whose time has not yet come. I am inclined to agree with him, for reasons best expressed by Walter Kerr in a *New York Times Magazine* article appearing one week before Mr. Papp's appointment was announced. It was Mr. Kerr's view that the presence of a fledgling company in a cultural complex that also housed such established institutions as the Met, the New York City Ballet, and the Philharmonic inevitably aroused expectations of quality that could not be quickly realized, especially since the best American actors were not inclined to join the company. Speculating that the same actors might very well be enticed into single plays in limited runs, Mr. Kerr concluded by calling for a single-play approach at the Beaumont pretty much along the lines later announced by Mr. Papp.

I suspect that such *en suite* projects probably constitute the most workable answer to the American need for an instant theatre culture, the only other alternative being a booking-house solution. But the disturbing thing about Mr. Kerr's argument is the way he proceeds to generalize from the example of Lincoln Center and conclude that because a permanent company is "an impossible dream" in official culture centers, it is also undesirable anywhere else in New York, and even (if I read him correctly) in the rest of metropolitan America. Not only do I disagree with this, I believe it is a prescription for the end of serious American theatre, for I have no doubt whatever that there is no sensible alternative to repertory if theatre is going to survive in this country as a viable artistic medium.

Mr. Kerr's arguments against repertory (they are also expressed by my old friend, Stanley Kauffmann, in a recent *New Republic* article) take the following form. (1) The repertory system is designed for the development of actors rather than the enjoyment of audiences, and (Kerr) "audiences will not support repertory simply because it is good for actors." (Kauffmann adds: "American audiences have been conditioned to expect prominent virtuosos or, at least, personalities in a cast, rather than an ensemble of putatively equal merit and blended personalities.") (2) Permanent companies demand of actors a period of residence and a share of commitment, but "The Best," as Kerr calls them, "are offered too much exciting variety in their own careers to want to settle into any nest, however cozy." (3) "Theatre audiences are now accustomed, in a metropolis, to choosing among theatres, not among plays in one theatre" (Kauffmann), and (Kerr) "New York . . . is itself a repertory operation" by virtue of its manifold offerings ("30 Broadway and God-knows-how-many off-Broadway entertainments each week"). (4) American society is not responsive to permanent theatres, because, in Stanley Kauffmann's phrase, "the whole social-cultural drift is against repertory."

Let me try to answer these objections, one by one.

1. *The system is designed for developing actors, not for entertaining audiences who usually prefer stars.* Although there is some truth in this observation, it is true only of certain kinds of audiences, generally those who patronize Broadway. In its brief career thus far, the American repertory system has developed an entirely different kind of spectator with new habits of mind (I wish it could develop some new habits among critics as well), capable of enjoying an actor's move-

ment from one role to another, as well as appreciating the ensemble work of a company and the organic links between its plays. I know such satisfactions are real, because I have seen people enjoying them. (Needless to say, I enjoy them myself.) And if this occasionally means tolerating an unfinished performance for the sake of a later breakthrough, well . . . the mark of a mature society is its capacity to defer immediate gratifications. By what other process will actors grow?

I confess that I am rather impatient with the argument from the audience's point of view, especially in such a degraded form as the American theatre. It puzzles me why theatre critics so often make the desires of the audience the basis for their own expectations and conclusions when these desires are of so little moment among critics of serious music, painting, poetry, and fiction. This is an inheritance of Broadway thinking, with its logic of the box office, and it suggests why American theatre rises so rarely above the level of a commodity. Certainly audiences are essential to the survival of any serious theatre; but any serious theatre that concerns itself exclusively with the demands of the audience does not, in my opinion, deserve to survive.

2. *Actors have too much variety in their careers to want to stay with companies.* If this means variety of opportunities in the media, then I suppose it is true. If it means variety of artistic opportunities, then where is it true? On Broadway? In Alka-Seltzer commercials? *Hawaii Five-O? Easy Rider* or *Five Easy Pieces?* Any actor worthy of the name knows that genuine variety is possible only in repertory companies where he has the opportunity to play most of the great classical roles and many of the exciting new ones, without being forced to repeat his performance from one realistic vehicle to another.

What discourages many actors from repertory, I fear, is not the loss of variety, but the fear of losing out on the main chance (even though companies often make provision through temporary leaves for other kinds of work). I once invited an actor, then in Hollywood, to play a part in Ford's *'Tis Pity She's a Whore* at Yale. After first accepting, he then bowed out, informing me through his agent that he had just been given a terrific opportunity in a television pilot. The agent offered to send me the script to show why the actor couldn't possibly turn it down; I offered to send him a copy of Ford's play. Inevitably, the option on the pilot was not picked up, and the actor went back to wait around his swimming pool, while our play went on with a lesser actor in the role. Such examples could be multiplied a thousandfold.

3. *New York is a repertory theatre.* Yes, and it's also a summer festival. What is one to say to an argument like this when the New York theatre is in such a conspicuous state of deterioration? The thirty Broadway and countless off-Broadway shows mentioned by Mr. Kerr are a sign not of the theatre's health, but of its decline—I won't bother to quote the statistics; they are already too well known. London has quadruple the number of commercial offerings and about twenty times as many experimental productions, while supporting two major repertory companies (the National and the Royal Shakespeare Company) and five or six minor ones.

4. *The repertory system is against the whole social-cultural drift of the nation.* This strikes me as the best argument for supporting it. Among a few other things against the drift of the nation at the moment are decent poverty programs, help for our decaying cities, sensible drug legislation, honest business practices, and integrity in the highest reaches of government; in fact, the only thing I can think of that is not against the drift of the nation is . . . drift. It should not be necessary to tell theatre critics of liberal persuasion that life has no dynamic or purpose unless it pushes against the tide. Or, as Bernard Shaw put it, "To be in hell is to drift; to be in heaven is to steer."

So to those who say we cannot have subsidized permanent companies in America, my answer is *we must*—not only to resist the theatre's traditional egocentricity and careerism but to help counter the nation's indifference to change. If we can accomplish this small task, there is a hope that we can start to solve some of the larger problems of the country. For contrary to those who think support for the arts eats up resources that should be going to the poor, I think a healthy culture and a compassionate society are as closely linked as a sane mind and a sound body. My proof is England, which now takes care of the needs of all its people, through a comprehensive system of social services, at the same time that it subsidizes, among other valuable cultural expressions, some of the most distinguished repertory companies in the world.

The history of America in regard to the theatre has thus far been a scandal, and the majority of American actors have shared not a little in the disgrace. One thing is certain: there will be no serious theatre in this country without the active participation of the profession in the repertory movement, not to mention the understanding of critics regarding its goals and purposes. For this, the career of Diana Rigg stands witness, both as an example—and as a rebuke. (1973)

Window on the World
The World Theatre Festival

The World Theatre Season is soon to complete its tenth and final year at the Aldwych Theatre with the Zulu *Macbeth*, and Peter Daubeny, who has been running the Festival ever since he first conceived it, is among those on the birthday list receiving knighthoods from the Queen. Sir Peter's honors are richly deserved, for the appearance on these shores of companies from all over the world has been of incalculable value to those concerned about the possibilities of the theatre.

I don't mean, as is sometimes claimed for the Festival, that it constitutes a source of intercultural brotherhood and human communion where artists demonstrate to politicians how to make countries work peacefully together. As Sir Peter could undoubtedly attest from his difficulties in negotiating these international events, the vanity of theatre people has almost as much explosive potential as the ambitions of statesmen, and possibly even more propensity for retaliatory action when wounded. No, the primary importance of these visits is not political, since brotherly sentiments tend to wear off quickly, or even artistic, though the Festival can boast of significant achievements. I think it lies, rather, in the potential of the World Theatre Season to spread a sense of cultural humility. As one commentator hopefully puts it, the Festival has made the English people "more critical spectators. It has breached our snobbery and dented our insularity. We will now be not so easily pleased with our National Theatre and Royal Shakespeare Company."

Considering how easily national pride can turn into chauvinistic smugness, this is an important function indeed, especially now that England has entered the European community. A country needs a strong sense of identity, but it occasionally needs to measure this identity against that of other nations. England has come a long way since the time when Bernard Shaw used to satirize the narrow-mindedness of Roebuck Ramsden and other such imperial Victorians in blinkers, but it still shows traces of insular habits of mind, and nowhere more than in the theatre. Not long ago, for example, the critic for a leading Sunday newspaper called everybody a "clodhopper" who didn't think John Osborne's latest play a masterpiece, also remarking, in a subordinate clause of his *Misanthrope* review, that he disliked the whole of Molière. This is rather like the *Figaro* critic memorializing the latest product of M. Anouilh, at the same time proudly proclaiming his indifference to Shakespeare and abusing the rest of the nation for failing to share his eccentric views. If it only forces the English to challenge such provincial opinions and examine its local prejudices, the World Theatre Season will have done its job.

Still, it is difficult not to notice how many of the companies visiting London this year and in the past have been national or establishment theatres. One of the few American companies ever invited to the Festival, for example, was the star-studded but ill-fated Actors Studio Theatre, when a much more interesting choice in the sixties would have been the Open Theatre, especially during the heyday period of *America Hurrah*. (By coincidence, the Open Theatre is presently in London, performing at the Roundhouse in a disappointing program of three collective creations—*The Mutation Show, Night Walk,* and *Terminal*—which have met deservedly sour reviews.) This bias in favor of the well-established is only to be expected, since few companies could undertake such an expensive journey without substantial help, and the more experimental troupes seldom have the prestige to attract the necessary funds. On the other hand, the trouble with establishment companies is that they tend to have become rather stale by the time they have acquired support, while some of the national companies are inclined to avoid all risks in order to guarantee their government subsidies.

This certainly was my impression of the Comédie Française on its recent visit (though my judgment was made without having seen the popular *Richard III*, directed by the Royal Shakespeare Company's Terry Hands). Performing in two of Molière's medicine shows, the early *commedia Le Médecin Volant* and the late comedy-ballet *Le Malade Imaginaire,* the troupe showed its usual skill and accomplishment. But when acting becomes this conventionalized, it begins to look more like classical ballet. Even more frozen in traditionalism was the Vienna Burgtheater's stolid production of Schnitzler's *Liebelei,* while the Umewaka Noh Theatre from the East and Belgium's Rideau de Bruxelles from the West both managed to baffle the audience with their arcane gestures and impenetrable mysteries.

Considerably more available to audience understanding was the Bochum Schauspielhaus production of *Little Man, What Now,* a sentimental play with cabaret trappings about life in pre-Nazi Germany. But although the work was meant to embody some kind of comment on the corruptions of capitalism, it was almost staggering in its own affluent vulgarity, featuring a cast of forty, plus a female chorus of eleven, a large swing band in the wings, countless set changes, and innumerable costumes, including the entire stock of a men's-clothing store. I came away glutted by the experience, not so much admiring the company's talents as envying its apparently bottomless subsidy.

The Nuria Espert Company from Spain, in Lorca's *Yerma,* was greatly appreciated, and the performances were unquestionably virile and passionate. But the trampoline used in Victor García's production seemed to me a distracting novelty that called too much attention to its clumsy mechanics and created annoying obstacles for the actors. (Then, one was tempted to ask, why a trampoline rather than a Jungle Jim, or, for that matter, a kidney-shaped swimming pool?)

On the other hand, Ingmar Bergman's production of *The Wild Duck*, with Sweden's Royal Dramatic Theatre, electrified the season with a powerful (if curiously straightforward) interpretation of Ibsen's play. Certainly the performance was hardly noteworthy for its physical production. The lighting was so dim you couldn't tell which of the actors was wearing whiskers, and the settings were surprisingly seedy, considering Bergman's visual acumen in the films. The first-act scene in Gregers Werle's house consisted of a few armchairs and a badly painted portrait of his mother, while Hjalmar's house was a shallow horizontal platform, entered by a door that squeaked and sometimes failed to latch, and bordered by two scruffy leafless trees on Christmas stands. (And why was the Werle room painted green when it is the Ekdal household that is supposed to be under water?)

But who could complain, when Bergman was able to coax such marvelous performances from his company? Emphatically an actor's director in the theatre, Bergman created considerable pathos in his handling of the heartbroken Hedvig (whose physical relationship with her father seemed to go well beyond the filial) and the good-humored, stoical Gina. But the evening clearly belonged to Max von Sydow, as Gregers Werle, and Ernst-Hugo Jaregard, as Hjalmar Ekdal. Von Sydow's Gregers was an incredibly awkward, stooped, and self-conscious ogre, his lank hair hanging like limp flax, his body hugged into pretzel-like contortions as he poured his destructive idealism into Ekdal's ears. And Jaregard carefully built Ekdal into a hollow man and posturing fraud, self-important, declamatory, and appetitive, the perfect embodiment of the histrionic self. These performances Bergman modulated with the modesty and confidence of a fine conductor, bringing each character, however minor, to his emotional fulfillment.

This performance alone would have justified this year's

World Theatre Season. But it was surpassed by something
even finer, the Cracow Stary Theatre production of Dostoevsky's *The Possessed,* in the Camus adaptation as revised by the
director Andrzej Wajda. Wajda (known best through his work
in films) combined, with this Polish company, the fundamental
techniques of Stanislavski with the most imaginative post-
Stanislavski innovations—histrionic truth coupled with unpredictability and surprise, directorial control that expands
and reinforces the source material while treating it in an
entirely original way, scenic momentum that moves the play
with the speed of a comet, yet permits the spectator to absorb
its full impact—thus providing a synthesis of two usually
divergent theatrical movements.

Wajda placed his production against a dead sky on a floor
made of mud—mud that had dried into blisters and boils, and
caked on the bottoms of trousers and the hems of dresses.
Within this barren landscape, the set pieces were changed to
the accompaniment of harrowing electronic sounds by a sinister chorus completely covered in black linen—a chorus that
gradually enveloped and controlled the action like tutelary
demons. And what a pace he set! From the moment Stavrogin
began the play, rattling off a confession in a fever of self-
loathing, until the moment he ended it by hanging himself in
a wardrobe, the production never flagged in the onward rush
of its hallucinated intensity.

Camus' adaptation is an intelligent but theatrically conventional work that preserves the arguments of Dostoevsky's
novel at the cost of its character development; Wajda's revision fills in the characters as well in sure deft strokes.
Dostoevsky's gallery of the damned are all present, and in all
their similarity to certain extreme contemporary types: the
parasitical liberal Stepan Verkhovensky; the engineer Kirilov,
proving his Godhead through a meaningless suicide; the humane student Shatov; the theorist Shigalov, expounding his
political dogma to an inflamed revolutionary cell ("I begin
in complete freedom and end in complete despotism. . . . That
is my despair"); and, most important, the bored nihilist
Stavrogin, and his hideous admirer, the rabid terrorist Peter
Verkhovensky.

All the acting in this extraordinary production had a terrifying air of heightened reality, as if Wajda had discovered the stage equivalent of the film close-up. But Jan Nowicki, as Stavrogin, and Wojchiech Pszoniak, as Peter, were especially electrifying—the one rigid with despair, his eyes blazing with brain fever, a mirthless smile flickering across his face, the other biting his nails in high excitement or scooting across the stage diagonally like a huge decapitated chicken. These performances the director supplemented with vivid stage images: Stepan dying on the ground near a broken wagon on which sits a black-robed figure like a mournful vulture; Stavrogin and Peter joining in a gentle Russian folk song after having agreed to murder one of their cell; the Narrator desperately trying to conclude the story, after Stavrogin's suicide, only to have his mouth stopped by the hands of the chorus. In short, a landmark production that confirms, in one fell swoop, the primacy of the theatre as a medium of philosophy in action and immediate sensuous experience.

This is the kind of work that, if performed in America, would have instantly caused five or six groups to spring up in imitation; yet in London it was politely received by a partially empty house, and though it appeared at last year's Festival, too, it has had no discernible influence on the English stage. This says much about the openness of the American theatre as contrasted with the complacency of the English—or perhaps about British confidence compared with American insecurity. Either way you look at it, the theatres of both countries have their problems; but it's only by the measure of such stunning standards that problems like these are likely to be identified and solved. (1973)

The Prevalence of Style
The Cherry Orchard

How ungracious I've been this season about the English theatre, and its more highly praised staples! I sometimes feel like the dyspeptic guest at the family dinner complaining about the cuisine while everyone else is toasting the chef. Well, I'll soon be putting my napkin back in its ring, to the audible relief of many at the table; but before I leave the dining room, it's only fair to explain by what standards I've been finding this year's theatrical fare somewhat less than appetizing.

In judging production, three qualities seem to be important: (1) *emotional texture*, or the depth and penetration of performance, (2) *imaginative daring*, or the exercise of the intelligent fancy in conceptualizing texts, and (3) *style*, or the skill and polish that bring a production up to professional pitch. I have listed these qualities in what I consider to be their proper order of importance; which is to say, on a descending scale from internal reality to external accomplishment. The emotional texture of a production leaves the most lasting mark on the spectator; imaginative daring stimulates his mind and impresses him with a sense of the artist's uniqueness; and style arouses his admiration for technical craftsmanship and dexterity.

The really memorable works of the theatre usually possess all three of these qualities in abundance—a recent example is the Cracow Stary Theatre production of *The Possessed*. But perfectly sound productions can be created on the basis of only one. The question is which one. If style is the predominant feature of the theatre over a long period, it can produce a trivializing effect. And if I sense triviality in much recent English theatre, it may be because I think it has grown too dependent on style. Obviously, a stylistic attack is essential to the production of certain kinds of plays, notably comedies of wit and farces, which English companies do superlatively well. But when technical adroitness becomes the hallmark of the theatre as a whole, it may cease to provide enough nourishment to sustain growth.

What accounts for the prevalence of style at the expense of passion and adventure on the current English stage? One can start to generalize an answer on the basis of such national characteristics as British reserve (to account for the absence of passion) or verbal fluency (to account for the dominance of style), but this would clearly be wrong, for until very recently the English stage was distinguished by many productions that displayed power as well as skill, daring along with accomplishment. One thinks of Peter Brook's work, particularly *Lear* and *Marat/Sade,* or of Peter Hall's antiwar *Henry V* with Ian Holm, of Olivier's *Othello,* Scofield's *Government Inspector,* or the fine productions at the Court under George Devine. And one thinks, too, of John Gielgud's infinitely funny and touching 1954 version of *The Cherry Orchard.*

I suspect the answer lies in the audience, for whom style is assumed to be the most readily accessible quality in the theatre; and as evidence of this, let me cite Michael Blakemore's production of *The Cherry Orchard* at the National. By contrast with Gielgud's version, this interpretation is largely an exercise in style. It is civilized, glamorous, sophisticated, well thought out, and carefully paced, packed with stage business and sound effects—and rather anemic of imagination, starved of emotional matter. One feels the hand of a professional in every nook and cranny; what one doesn't feel is the cumulative impact of the play.

I think the production is attempting to please the audience too much at the expense of the author. In the third-act ballroom scene, for example, Mr. Blakemore has organized a handsome interlude, with the richly wardrobed guests swirling about the stage so gracefully that their dance elicits applause from the audience. But the social events of this decaying house are not meant to recall the choreography of *The Great Waltz;* actually, things have grown so seedy that, as old Firs tells us, the family is hardly able to count on the attendance of the postal clerk and the stationmaster, neither of whom would be distinguished by his dancing or his tailoring.

The disintegration of this once-noble household is not suggested often by the actors either, since Constance Cummings's charming and attractive Mme. Ranevskaya never sufficiently establishes an affectionate relationship with her rooms and furnishings. (The Moscow Art Ranevskaya actually embraced the furniture when she entered and kissed the walls.) And the director's decision to revolve the stage in the last scene, showing Firs trapped in a cell-like room, squeezes extra pathos for this character at the cost of diminishing the importance of the entire house as a central image of loss and desolation.

Then, Denis Quilley's Lopakhin, embodying style in abundance, is played not as a clumsy good-hearted peasant who bumps into furniture and flails his arms about, but rather as an elegant, well-mannered businessman, possibly modeled on an executive of Lonrho. And while Michael Hordern is so cuddly as Gayev that I felt the impulse to hug him, his winsome, winking Hulot figure is some distance from the cranky, vacant, and somewhat snobbish character Chekhov wrote.

Other performances disappoint for similar reasons, notably Maggie Riley as Charlotte, an actress who has mastered the ventriloquistic skills of this eccentric German while ignoring her *eins-zwei-drei* preciseness and hidden loneliness, and Gillian Barge as Varya, an appealing and willowy maiden instead of a nunnish spinster. I enjoyed watching Louise Purnell's flighty Dunyasha, however, along with Anna Carteret's pink-cheeked Anya, and David Bradley's Trofimov, played like a radical student from the London School of Economics; I found Ronald Hingley's translation both flowing and colloquial; and I was grateful to Mr. Blakemore for the considerable comedy he was able to evoke from the play, particularly in the first act. This director has demonstrated once again that he is a skilled craftsman of the stage. Now I hope he will begin to grapple a little more painfully with the inner demons of the plays.

For only then will he recall to us what theatre is at its best:

not a demonstration of brilliance and elegance, not an easy route to the approval of the spectator, not a civilized escape from everyday cares, all of which are the attractions of style, but a brave exploration of the inner labyrinths of human character as revealed in a crisis of action.   (1973)

The Contemporary English Theatre: Mirror or Lamp?

From all outward appearances, the London Theatre would seem to be in a state of flourishing health; plays continue to pour into theatres at the rate of five or six a week, and audiences flock to most of them with eagerness and anticipation.

But after nine months in this capital, I am gnawed by a suspicion that everything is not as satisfactory as it appears on the surface. Ultimately, a nation's art is judged not quantitatively but qualitatively, and the theatre's capacity to entertain the spectator becomes of less moment than its capacity to stretch his mind, engage his emotions, and challenge his imagination. If the aspiration is low, it doesn't matter a whit in the long run whether the majority of audiences are being satisfied or an army of actors being employed, for a single individual in an isolated country—say, Ibsen in Norway—is sometimes of infinitely more importance to theatre history than a whole nation's active theatre over a period of years—say, France in the nineteenth century. Is the English theatre really serious? Does it aspire not only to amuse but to create seminal works of art? Certainly some of its critics think so; and Harold Hobson of the Sunday *Times* can usually be depended upon weekly to proclaim some new masterpiece of the British stage. My position is somewhat more equivocal. To judge from the past season, there is something wrong with the British theatre at present that no amount of critical cheer-leading is going to conceal; and I don't think it is going to build on its potential for greatness until some of the problems have been more openly acknowledged.

Certainly the 1972–73 season proved disappointing in all its major areas of activity. The commercial managements on Shaftesbury Avenue have never been known for daring, but this year they seemed even more timid than usual, paralyzing patrons with transvestite revues, overproduced American musicals, superficial sex comedies, star-studded revivals, and waxen soap operas about royalty. To be sure, Peter Cook and Dudley Moore tried to revive the art of the satiric revue with *Behind the Fridge,* but, as its parasitic title suggests, the show was a mere shadow of the imaginative frolic that inspired it, while Alan Bennett's *Habeas Corpus*—a witty romp by another Fringe alumnus—succeeded largely as a happy entertainment, despite belated efforts to establish a serious theme.

The serious play, in fact (by which I mean a play with serious intentions, regardless of its tone), seems virtually to have disappeared from the West End, as it already has from Broadway. Colin Welland's *Say Goodnight to Grandma* touched some deeper chords in its treatment of an amiable young sod devoured by his womenfolk, but it remained essentially a domestic comedy in a television format, while Ronald Mavor's *A Private Matter* and John Mortimer's *Collaborators,* though touching on potentially interesting issues, never transcended their limitations as witty exercises in style. The only play of genuine interest to appear all season on the West End, in fact, was Ibsen's *A Doll's House,* which had a freshness that belied its age, thanks largely to Claire Bloom's poignant performance in the part of Nora.

The Fringe, by contrast, is supposed to be defined by seriousness as well as by innovation—but I am afraid I found most of the Fringe work not serious but solemn, not so much innovative as raucous and exhibitionistic.

While it is difficult to generalize accurately about such a variegated phenomenon, the Fringe usually offers two distinct kinds of activity: the American-inspired improvisational groups who like to do their acting exercises in front of audiences, and presentations of the "Messages First" variety, with their scatter-shot barrage of statistics, strike threats, righteous indignation, and bald political rhetoric.

The most promising Fringe work, on the other hand, is usually done by isolated and unclassifiable groups—nomadic companies like the Low Moan Spectacular, applying a zany imagination to works with such titles as *El Grande de Coca-Cola* and *Bullshot Crummond,* and such permanent theatres as the Open Space, the Theatre Upstairs, the King's Head, and the Almost Free. These theatres are as dependable as their offerings—which is to say, they vary widely in quality—but such projects as Peter Handke's *Kaspar* (Almost Free), Caryl Churchill's *Owners* (Theatre Upstairs), Büchner's *Woyzeck* (Open Space), Fugard's *Hello and Goodbye* (King's Head), and Sam Shepard's *The Unseen Hand* (Theatre Upstairs) proved among the more interesting events of the London season, though only Miss Churchill's sensitive play could be called an authentic product of the English theatre.

As for the best resident and company theatres—the National, the Royal Shakespeare Company, the Royal Court— these have always been the glory of the English stage and the signal of its continuing vitality. Yet what seemed so vigorous and alive ten years ago now seems rather pallid and predictable, as the leadership of these companies has changed or, in some cases, failed to change enough.

The Royal Court, for example, is still responsible for most of the new English and Irish plays of any consequence, producing them every six weeks in the same prolific manner as it did under its founder, George Devine. Now under the supervision of the impresario Oscar Lewenstein, the Court— at the time of this writing—has already premiered plays by Brendan Behan, Edna O'Brien, John Osborne, Samuel Beckett, Brian Friel, Christopher Hampton, and Edward Bond, with one by David Storey still to come. This is an impressive list by any measure, so I feel almost churlish in remarking that the Court at present is lacking a persuasive sense of commitment or recognizable identity. George Devine used to produce plays because he believed in them, as well as in the people responsible for staging them; Mr. Lewenstein seems to produce them largely because they are available, using whatever performers might bring prestige to his theatre. As a result, most of the Court offerings this year have been lacking in genuine creative heat, and opportunities are seldom extended to new young playwrights, as Devine first did to Osborne, Wesker, and Arden.

To be sure, Billie Whitelaw performed Beckett's stunning *Not I* at the Court this year with such harrowing force and ferocity that she turned this fifteen-minute piece into one of the most shattering events of the entire season, and Edward Bond's *The Sea*, in William Gaskill's well-acted production, was an interesting new development for this fine, unpredictable writer. But Christopher Hampton's *Savages* and Brian Friel's *The Freedom of the City* both suffered from the substitution of political indignation for credible playwriting, perhaps on the assumption that if the audience shared some of the authors' outrage, they would not demand too much of their art, while John Osborne's *A Sense of Detachment* struck me as a peculiarly sterile exercise, the kind of doodle scrawled by writers while waiting for inspiration to flow.

Osborne contented himself with throwing six unrelated characters together on a bare stage, along with two well-rehearsed hecklers from the audience, and with a surprising lack of his customary bite, let them carry his opinions on such topics as women's liberation, the Irish troubles, and the fading glories of Britain, the last quarter of the evening being devoted almost entirely to recitations of English poetry juxtaposed with modern porn. The work had its admirers as well as its detractors, but it was too feeble even to be the occasion for a good theatrical row. Self-conscious, self-indulgent, arbitrary, and a little boozy, *A Sense of Detachment* was not so much a breakthrough as a breakdown, where even Osborne's experiments with form seemed weary and lackluster.

Whatever its capacity to fulfill them, the Royal Court at least is capable of raising one's expectations with its program, which is more than can be said, at the moment, for the National Theatre and the Royal Shakespeare Company. These companies are justly admired for their dash, expertise, charm, and efficiency; both of them generate more electricity than any establishment companies I know of (compare the frozen traditionalism of the Comédie Française); yet neither of them lately has been able to stage a truly memorable performance, one that probes and startles as well as dazzles and entertains.

Much has been written about the way the National has managed to redeem itself recently on the basis of such successful productions as Tom Stoppard's *Jumpers,* Michael Blakemore's investigations of American plays like *The Front Page* and *A Long Day's Journey into Night,* and John Dexter's updating of Molière's *The Misanthrope.* I would agree that all these productions are eminently worth seeing; but my point about English theatre in general, and the National in particular, is that quality is not to be measured by stylish "hits" so much as by adventurous exploits of the imagination, and by this standard the record of this theatre is not very distinguished. As Irving Wardle has described the current repertory at the National, "It was middlebrow entertainment at its most exhilarating, doing all the work for you and leaving you no time for reflection; least of all for reflecting on anything that touched on the state of modern Britain."

Mr. Wardle detected in his article (published last winter in the London *Times*) a note of smugness, complacency, and insularity in the British theatre, which he also found in the Royal Shakespeare Company. About the season of Roman plays produced at Stratford, Mr. Wardle charged that, although conceived in the same spirit as Peter Hall's War of the Roses series, it "lacked the contemporary application which lent such resonance to the English histories," while, concerning the Aldwych season of the RSC, he said: "Within the company there may be cogent reasons for reviving *Murder in the Cathedral* and *The Lower Depths,* and for continuing its Albee connection with the funereal *All Over.* But taken in conjunction with the Stratford season, these shows suggest that the RSC has temporarily lost contact with its public."

I am not certain that closer contact with an already admiring public is the key to the problems of the RSC, nor do I agree that its productions might be improved with the aid of more contemporary relevance. Certainly John Barton's production of *Richard II* proved an illuminating and original interpretation of a well-known play without recourse to modern social and political parallels, while the Aldwych's catastrophic production of the boring *Island of the Mighty,* by John Arden and Margaretta D'Arcy, was an unmitigated disaster, despite its obvious efforts to be socially aware and politically conscious.

I think Mr. Wardle is correct in seeing the problem as one of leadership, and I would extend this possibility to the English theatre at large: it is rich in professional competence but rather threadbare of vision and passion. Sir Laurence Olivier endowed the National company during his distinguished reign with his wisdom, stability, and personal artistry—but his interests were custodial rather than innovative, and, being a great actor himself, he was always more partial to large roles in anthology productions than to exciting new plays or venturesome new techniques. (As his literary manager, the gifted Kenneth Tynan commissioned some interesting new plays and translations, but the general level of the repertory was rarely much above that of a progressive West End management.) As for the RSC, Trevor Nunn, in taking over the reins from Peter Hall, unwittingly repealed the Brechtian reforms that formerly gave this company such muscularity, originality, and strength by substituting the kind of conventional programming and ornamental productions that Brecht used to call "culinary"—which is to say, easily consumed. And Peter Brook, who once conducted his brilliant explorations of texts within the context of the RSC, has apparently grown tired of written plays and coherent language, and is now experimenting with an invented tongue against the background of exotic environments.

What is most seriously missing from the English theatre at present is not a great creative talent—these are always in short supply—but an intelligent and fertile theatrical imagination. In a time of artistic drought, when the playwrights are hibernating, the theatre can always renew itself through adventurous programing, inventive ideas, and controversial approaches to classical material. But except for a handful of interesting productions this year, what we have been getting instead of creative daring are warmed-over repertory chestnuts, a few barbaric yawps from the Fringe, and a parade of cadavers from the embalming parlors on the West End.

Where hope is kept alive is in the insatiable appetite of the English audience for theatre. (When I went to a police station recently to have my employment permit validated, the officer on duty, noting my profession, engaged me in conversation about the theatre, and particularly about the Royal Court, where he and his wife are patrons; this encounter is almost unthinkable in America.) And the prospects brighten also in the work of a few playwrights—Edward Bond and Harold Pinter strike me as the most interesting—and in the appointment of Peter Hall as the new director of the National Theatre. As Mr. Hall proved during his period with the RSC, he is both an accomplished administrator and an inspiring director; and he has managed to surround himself at the National with some of the most gifted men on the English stage: Jonathan Miller, Michael Blakemore, John Schlesinger, and Harold Pinter as directors, and John Bury as resident designer. All these men are capable of doing important work in the right atmosphere; and one has every reason to believe that Mr. Hall will establish the right atmosphere at the National.

The best modern theatres—Antoine's Théâtre Libre, the Moscow Art Theatre under Stanislavski, the Court under Devine, the Berliner Ensemble under Brecht, the early Living Theatre—have always functioned not as mirrors reflecting the taste of the audience, but rather as lamps lighting the way to new directions. If Peter Hall can resist the inevitable pressures to make the National a mirror of existing British culture—if he can extend his hospitality to the most exciting talents England can offer, regardless of their appeal for audiences—then he is in an excellent position to bring the English theatre once more to a position of eminence, to make it a place that is not just likable and entertaining but illuminating and profound. (1973)

Back to the Wilderness
The Open Theatre

The Open Theatre, first and foremost among the American performing groups that flowered in the sixties, is back in London for a brief period. After its return to the United States for a final tour in the autumn, it plans to disband. There is sadness in this announcement, and some cultural significance, too, for the history of this innovative troupe has spanned —and in certain ways reflected—a period of great turbulence in the United States.

My own experience of the Open Theatre goes back ten years to the time when the company first exposed its experiments to an invited audience in New York's Martinique Hotel. I remember feelings of respect, tempered with puzzlement and a little apprehension. I admired the discipline with which American actors were completing difficult physical and vocal tasks, but I was puzzled by the apparent irrelevance of these abstract exercises to any coherent artistic purpose, and vaguely dismayed by the oddly dehumanized quality of the sounds and gestures. With the production of *America Hurrah* in 1967, however, the purpose of the experiments seemed to become clear, for the mechanistic style of the Open Theatre's acting proved admirably suited to Jean-Claude van Itallie's vision of American society as a brutalized machine. In that moment, the American theatre enjoyed a synthesis of writing and production that had not been equaled since the early days of the Group Theatre.

So compelling was this work, in fact, that for a while it looked as though our theatre were poised on the brink of a genuine renaissance. Alas, that new birth was soon to be aborted by the continuing savagery of a senseless war and by its deteriorating effect upon an increasingly desperate society.

In the theatre, this effect could be seen in the chaotic, mindless, arrogant antics of the many radical groups that followed in the Open Theatre's wake—in the opportunism of Schechner's Performance Group, in the anti-verbal calisthenics of La Mama, in the audience manipulation of the Living Theatre, and, not least of all, in the revolutionary playacting performed on the stage of the university in the form of endless disruptions, occupations, and confrontations.

Virtually all these groups (the radical students excepted) had mastered the physical control and technical discipline that distinguished the work of the Open Theatre; but most of their presentations, though offered as a healthy response to the diseased American imagination, looked more like a symptom than a cure. In particular, the Living Theatre returned to the United States in 1968 (having spent some years in European exile after a brilliant early career) flaunting the same repressive, irrational, vaguely totalitarian qualities as the country that had originally caused its departure. And flaunting a similar philistinism, too, since it was now rejecting any theatre that had not evolved from the personal experience of the company, and substituting sensationalism, anti-intellectualism, self-righteousness, and a disguised but ravenous hunger for publicity.

During this depressing time, the Open Theatre (under the tireless, almost monastic supervision of Joseph Chaikin) remained devoted to the development of its artistic process, and to its announced goal of "making visible the human situation at a time 'when things could be different.'" Implicit in this statement was a social-aesthetic concern for inventing theatrical metaphors that would accurately mirror the American condition; implicit also was a muted political activism that was to find expression not so much in didactic works as in underlying sentiments, in the choice of subject matter rather than in exhortations to action. Still, if the group never again managed to realize the promise of *America Hurrah* except in fits and starts, it may have been for a political reason—an obsession with the "collective" that prevented the group from subordinating its interests to the "autocracy" of a single informing mind.

In *America Hurrah,* the Open Theatre was able to bring a developed technique to an already written text, as the Moscow Art Theatre did to *The Seagull*; but in most of its succeeding productions the writer was treated simply as another citizen in a democratic state where everybody contributed equally. The result was the evolution of group activity without an overview—scattered fragmentary moments that lacked a formal imagination to give them direction and point. This approach was no doubt eminently satisfying to the performers, and unquestionably created intense feelings of loyalty to the group. But what makes a person happy in his work is not the same as what makes the work happy; and the fact is that actors, no matter how gifted, are not prepared to create as well as to enact harmonious and meaningful plays. The dancer had begun to confuse himself with the dance; the company's unity of style was paid for in the coin of self-indulgence, disjointed scenes, and grab-bag moments.

The defects and the virtues of the Open Theatre are now on view at the Roundhouse, in a three-work cycle beginning with the "collective creation" called *The Mutation Show.* This show demonstrates once again that the Open Theatre is a well-coordinated organism; but the evening is so lacking in any formal coherence that even its sixty-minute length seems a little tiresome. *The Mutation Show* propels eight actors onto the stage in various degrees of spasm, epilepsy, aphasia, and cretinism, and proceeds to identify them as circus side-show freaks (The Bird Lady, The Man Who Smiles, The Man Who Hits Himself, The Petrified Man, and so on). What follows is not so much the development of this idea as its extension—or, rather, its *mutation*—as the characters transform themselves into various species of grotesques, sighing, wheezing, screaming, groaning, and straining their bodies into several distorted shapes.

Occasionally, a coherent idea breaks loose from this freak show, or an interesting image; one actor emerges from a box, sightless and covered with uterine blood; the whole ensemble performs a spasmodic wedding dance to the "Anniversary Waltz," which a caller turns into a capsule history of the last ten years ("The bride is now dancing with the mother of the groom. . . . The President is now dancing with his assassin. . . . The oilmen are now dancing with the Vietnamese"). But the ideas seem rather banal, and even a few years out-of-date (odd for a company so devoted to process), when they don't appear to be looted from better works.

The spirit of Peter Handke seems to hover over this piece, particularly in an episode involving an "animal girl" who, like Kaspar, is wrenched from an innocent state and mutilated by language ("We will name her. We will give her words. We will strengthen her bones. We will caress her"), but the assumption that society destroys instinct by means of speech seems no less sentimental here, where it even lacks Handke's form and eloquence. An unmistakably serious and intense evening, yet one that rarely transcends a certain self-satisfaction with its own technique.

In *Night Walk*, the Open Theatre boasts the participation of three good writers—Sam Shepard, Jean-Claude van Itallie, and Megan Terry—but since the performance contains very little coherent dialogue, it is likely that their contributions were voted down in the last general elections. Now and then, a line or two is heard above the din of bleats and chicken noises (typical example: "You are the absence I have lived with always"), but they are generally too pretentious to be quoted without blushing. This "work-in-progress" was begun as an exploration of "the levels of sleep," but aside from a few characters taking snoozes on the stage, and another saying "Gottagetgetgetget-gottagetgetgetup," it seems only faintly connected with the unconscious.

There is some unity created through the design, as the cast is rolled on stage from behind a screen on wheeled trolleys, reminding one sometimes of medieval mansions and sometimes of the chairs with which inmates are pushed around the grounds of a madhouse. There are a considerable number of animal exercises, idiot noises, calisthenics, a little singing, a snatch of poetry, some obscene clowning—and some of this is funny—but too often the cast reminded me of gifted kids doing prepared pieces in front of company. And there is a note of intolerable superiority about some of the scenes, particularly a satire on bourgeois table conversations that comes off like Jackie Gleason's *Honeymooners* being performed by autistic children. In short, the Open Theatre used to provide us with images of American society in disintegration; now these metaphors seem to be disintegrating, too, thus proving that we're all in this thing together.

Finally, there is a certain melancholy symmetry in the fact that my last column as guest reviewer for the *Observer* should be devoted to an American troupe. My first in this space, which discussed American influences on certain Fringe groups, was called, "I Never Left Home." This last one suggests that, in some disquieting sense, home has never left me. The chaotic nature of our lives in America, and the fragmented nature of the theatre that reflects it, is nowhere better illustrated than in the present work of this enterprising group. But I will not try to hide the sense of foreboding with which I leave your stable society, with its eloquent and homogeneous theatre, to enter once again the American wilderness. I have cherished the opportunity to be among you, despite my several cavils and complaints. And I leave with the warmest feelings of pleasure and regret, sustained by the hope that someday I may return.   (1973)

3
Back Again

The Profession Is Not
Supporting the Profession!

It is no news, of course, that there is a crisis in the American theatre, particularly theatre in New York, which has been deteriorating steadily since the end of World War II. This crisis seems particularly acute when you return, as I just have, from England, a country where the appetite for theatre is voracious, where London alone produces four to eight new plays each week. If you look at the New York theatre directory, you'll notice that it advertises only eighteen productions, of which only eight are truly the property of Broadway; the rest belong either to off-Broadway or to the institutional theatres in which they originated.

Think of it—only eight Broadway productions held over from the previous season and only eighteen theatres operating! When you calculate that each of these Broadway theatres holds on average about a thousand spectators, you will notice a dismaying statistic: at the close of the summer, only eighteen thousand people can find accommodation each night in the commercial theatre—a figure that represents little over one-fifth of 1 percent of the population of a city of eight million. New York may be a summer festival, but if so, the festivities no longer seem to include many plays.

The crisis is so marked that it has now begun to trouble even Broadway's most faithful supporters, among them Walter Kerr, who concluded in a recent article that in order to survive, the commercial theatre would have to move to the upper East Side. This proposal proceeded logically from his assumption that there's nothing wrong with Broadway that a safer neighborhood wouldn't cure, which is neat in the way it makes the whole problem a matter of environment.

No doubt it is possible to find some correlation between the deterioration of Broadway as a neighborhood and the failure of the theatre there, but surely other causes are responsible, too, including some aesthetic ones. If New Yorkers were really passionate about Broadway fare, I think they would be willing to circumnavigate a street full of muggers and hookers, as the Elizabethans once braved ruffians and whores in order to see the plays of Marlowe and Shakespeare. Certainly Joe Papp doesn't have much trouble locating audiences, even though the Public Theatre is ensconced in the East Village, surely one of the most squalid neighborhoods in the city. No, the root causes of the problem lie elsewhere—in spiraling costs, formula producing, audience indifference—and they are not going to vanish by moving Neil Simon's goods to Third Avenue and Sixty-sixth Street.

Actually, most of the interesting works being produced in New York are the products of permanent institutional theatres—among them, the Public Theatre, the Negro Ensemble Company, Circle in the Square, the Phoenix, the Chelsea, and the American Place in New York; and outside of New York, the Guthrie, the Arena Stage, the Long Wharf, and the Mark Taper. And while it is contrary to our own laboratory policy to use our theatre as a pre-New York tryout house, the Yale Repertory Theatre has functioned in a similar tributary fashion, funneling a large number of its plays, productions, and techniques into the American theatre at large—and attracting in the process large numbers of young spectators once thought to be permanently lost to the movies.

But even more than plays, it is people who make their mark upon the American theatre—and I am thinking not of the many gifted professionals who have worked with resident companies over the years, but rather of the students who have been graduated from the various professional training centers. While some of these people can be seen on and off Broadway, most of them have chosen to work with institutional theatres— which is not surprising, considering the emphasis of their training—and their impact is being felt throughout the entire country, as directors, actors, designers, managers, technicians, playwrights, and literary managers.

But have the young people from such conservatories managed to change the face of the theatre—or merely to change some of the faces working in it? Will these young professionals arrive in sufficient time and sufficient force to keep the ship afloat, and function as exemplary models for other theatre people? The work done in these schools has been designed not just to train talented people in the techniques of their craft, but also to encourage them to demand a higher theatrical art and a more selfless professionalism than the theatre has shown in recent times. Are we realizing this goal, which is essentially an ethical goal, or is the American theatre losing its chance at honorable survival? Certainly the great majority of recent graduates seem to be working with dignity and commitment in their chosen profession; but I must confess that I don't yet see any conspicuous change in the ethical nature of the American stage.

To put it bluntly, the profession is not supporting the profession. People work in it, live at it, rise by it, but they don't seem to support it. Those who function in the theatre—and here I mean particularly actors—only rarely appear devoted to their profession above all things, or willing to sacrifice some of their personal career demands in order to help it survive.

Our own theatre season is about to open, and we are pleased to have assembled an excellent company of dedicated, talented professionals. But the sad fact is that for every actor who is willing to commit himself to the pursuit of art in repertory, another hundred continue to pursue the will-o'-the-wisp of personal aggrandizement, with consequences that frequently benefit neither the actor nor the theatre. After another summer spent trying to cast a season and hearing the same set responses—the same "Gee, I'd love to, but I can't afford it" or "I'm waiting on a pilot" or "I'm up for a movie" or "Can I let you know in March?" or "I'll come for a few weeks if you let me play Cyrano"—along with the same demands from agents that the actor have his name above the title or special songs written for him in the show, I still find it dispiriting that a performer could turn down a series of challenging roles in important plays, earning a good steady living among a community of artists, for a swipe at a TV series, a film, or a small part in the musical version of *Valley of the Dolls*. It's rather like a writer with ambitions to be a novelist who takes a job in advertising to pay the rent, and grows so used to the income that he can't give up writing copy even after a publisher offers him a contract for a book. By abandoning their early dreams for the sake of easy routes to wealth and fame, too many of these actors end up turning a temporary expedient into a permanent surrender, forgetting what brought them into the theatre in the first place.

I am reminded of an article called "Selling Out to Hollywood, or Home Is Where the Work Is," which recently appeared in the Arts and Leisure section of the *Times*. Written by a gifted naturalistic actress named Lee Grant, it described with considerable poignancy how she came to give up the theatre for the movies—only in Hollywood, she said, did she have the opportunity to act. The piece was filled with remorse—Miss Grant obviously has considerable affection for the theatre—and seemed persuasive until you stopped to think that there were a hundred places in the resident theatre movement where she might have continued to work, were she really serious about remaining in the theatrical profession. I had a sneaking suspicion that Miss Grant was feeling betrayed not so much by the theatre as a whole as by Broadway, which was failing to offer its customary opportunities. And so it was inevitable that she would eventually move her household to the very fount of stardom, there to commune with all the other expatriate New York actors about the death of the theatre and the boring California weather.

But the theatre isn't Broadway exclusively and, far from dying, it might well be in the process of renewing itself. For the very attractions that are now disappearing from the commercial stage—the "bright lights" mystique of fame and fortune—have been among the greatest obstacles to the development of a serious dramatic art in America, where the theatre has hitherto been an extension of business, supported by gamblers in the hope of a quick return on an investment.

The decline in the fortunes of the American theatre is opening it at last to possibility and development, for it is changing its shape and purpose as it loses its opportunities for self-aggrandizement. It is also losing a lot of its professionals in the process, and only time will tell whether it will flounder without them or whether enough dedicated young people will be able to provide it with the values to continue. What I foresee, then, is a race between those who are leaving and those who are coming to replace them. The outcome is still uncertain, but I have confidence the vacuum will be filled: professionals must begin to support their own profession.

The profession doesn't support the profession when actors permit agents to guide their lives and control their careers. It doesn't support the profession when they behave like unionized workers quarreling with management instead of like collaborators involved in a common artistic enterprise. It doesn't support the profession when they hold themselves more important than their material, or remain ignorant of the great works they should be serving. It doesn't support the profession when they give up on hard work, fierce discipline, and continual growth for the sake of easy alternatives. And it doesn't support the profession when they abandon the theatre for work that is often shallow, slack, and sleazy.

I don't wish to minimize the difficulties of the choices I propose, but I have just returned from a country where the profession is supported—and respected—by its actors, whose allegiance is first and foremost to the stage. It is a country, mind you, where television and films are generally of a much higher quality than one finds here, so that it would be relatively easy for English actors to rationalize careers in the media instead of on the stage. But the fact is that the senior actors in England—Olivier, Scofield, Richardson, Redgrave, Sim, Gielgud—set an example of theatrical commitment for the junior ones. Few leave the stage for long; most spend a substantial portion of the year with companies; and the handful that desert do so with considerable feelings of shame.

It is this quality of shame that seems to be missing from our own culture, probably because we put so much emphasis on success, and so little on what we are being successful at. It's not hard to see where this kind of pragmatism has led us, right up to the doors of Watergate, and it doesn't take much imagination to see its extension in the society at large. Some years ago, in an exuberant mood, some Americans were proclaiming a Woodstock nation. At this point in our history, it seems more accurate to call us a Watergate nation, for Americans of all kinds—young and old, culture and counterculture, men and women, politicians and artists—are somehow being scratched by the infected talons of that sorry eagle.

For what is Watergate but the culmination of the lies and deceptions, petty and gross corruptions, opportunism, anarchic pursuit of selfish goals, lack of scruples, power, lust, expediency, and hunger for success that have tainted postwar American life? The one positive lesson of Watergate is that poetic justice somehow continues to operate in our lives, for every person implicated in the scandal is suffering the destiny determined for him by his character. Won't the American theatre's destiny be determined by the characters of the people that work in it, too?

Watergate reveals that none of us commits an act in isolation, that every choice, no matter how insignificant, affects the quality of our national life, that everything we do and say will ultimately return to haunt us. The American theatre is now testing our characters, and the way we respond to that test will determine its future. If the profession fails, it has joined the Watergate nation, and helped to deliver our country over to its betrayers. To change the face of the theatre, then, we must try to change our own faces, keep faith with the dreams of our youth, and work to rekindle the light that once kept our hearts aflame.   (1973)

No More Masterpieces Revisited

*A Speech to the Shakespeare '74 Convention
at Brooklyn College*

Seven years ago, I wrote an article called "No More Master-pieces," in which I surprised myself—an erstwhile professor of dramatic literature—by coming out in favor of a much more elastic and radical approach to the classics than was being commonly practiced, particularly in producing Shake-speare. It seemed to me then that we had reached a turning point in our staging of such familiar works as *Hamlet, Macbeth,* and *A Midsummer Night's Dream,* and that the pious, reverential approach to Shakespeare then in vogue was in as much danger of putting dutiful husbands to sleep as Wagner-ian opera.

To remind you of my argument, I wrote that we had reached the end of a cycle in our staging of Shakespearean classics, and that we were desperately in need of renewal on the American stage similar to that being undertaken at the time in England.

The argument I advanced was that American classical theatre should begin to experiment with Shakespeare in ways similar to those being tried in England; and it is somewhat ironic at this moment, some seven years later, that not only has American theatre advanced along these lines, but it may have advanced a little too far, while English classical theatre seems to have retreated. It was with some dismay that I observed, in my capacity as a drama critic in London last year, the Royal Shakespeare Company, both at Stratford and at the Aldwych, cancelling the Brechtian revolution it had undergone under Peter Hall, and returning to the sumptuous, overproduced, overcostumed, somewhat declamatory Shake-speare left over from a previous age. This was particularly true of the Cecil B. de Mille-like *Titus Andronicus* I saw there in 1973, with its extravagant effects and its overemphasis on Stratford's new mechanical stage; and I don't suppose it was any accident that some of the new plays being produced at the Aldwych—notably John Arden's *Island of the Mighty,* a long-winded, overwritten Arthurian epic—reflected much the same gaudiness and excess in production.

The John Barton production of *Richard II* was something else again, because it was graced by a strong and intelligent informing idea; but even this good production was, in my opinion, marred by a sumptuous physical production, a far cry from the really startling originality and understatement of Peter Brook's productions with that company in the past. The productions of Shakespeare at the RSC, coupled with those I saw at the National Theatre and in some of the regional repertory companies, suggested that once again English Shakespearean production was becoming overly preoccupied with externals, with outsides, with appearances, and had momentarily lost sight of what Lear had called the "thing itself."

In the United States, on the other hand, the thing itself was also in eclipse; and since I have been commissioned to talk about American Shakespeare production, and most particularly Shakespeare production at the Yale Repertory Theatre, where I work, perhaps I had better get off this indelicate—not to say ungrateful—discussion of the English, and turn to our own faults and foibles. For the fact is that the new look at Shakespeare in this country has been attempted by a number of directors and companies, and the cry of "No more masterpieces," bawled out by myself, among others, has been answered perhaps to an extent originally unanticipated and undesired.

I would prefer not to cite specific examples, but rather to suggest the several radical approaches to Shakespeare that I find personally interesting, and others that leave me with less enthusiasm. In the latter category, I would cite the process, common to much institutional Shakespeare, known as "jollying up," which was basically a form of streamlining purely for novelty's sake.

A more recent approach to modernized Shakespeare was

that of the Performance Group, who generally improvised their own scenes and characters on the basis of the momentary psychic or political needs of the company members. This is the kind of classical production associated with Richard Schechner's company, with the Living Theatre, and with some of the Shakespeare experiments of Joe Papp, beginning, I suspect, with his own production of *Hamlet* some six years ago. The impulse behind that particular evening was courageous enough—to rescue the play from the seminar room, to withdraw it from history, to obliterate the memory of all those beautifully spoken, handsomely costumed productions of the play that now stand like a wall between us and the immediate experience of the action. But while I respected the bravery of this, and of many of the attempts that followed, mere irreverence was not enough to sustain the evening, because even absurdity has to be organized toward some recognizable point. The trouble with these Shakespeares, in my opinion, was that they contained too much of the spirit of the time and not enough of its mind, while the self-expression of the directors and actors, substituted for the intentions of the author, always bordered dangerously close on self-indulgence.

Here it is time to disclose my own particular bias, which I have not been concealing very effectively, for Shakespeare productions that function as poetic metaphors, excavating new entrances to the heart of the play. My objection to academic Shakespeare is that it reduces great plays to conventionalities, lulling us with the familiar and creating studied artificialities instead of immediate sensual experiences, and more and more I have come to believe that the mortal sin of the theatre—perhaps its only major sin—is to be boring.

But I have an objection to radical Shakespeare, too, whenever it threatens to substitute another form of externality for the significant heart of the theme and of the action. It has been said of Shakespeare that it was not of an age, but for all time. It is the job of modern producers to discover, as selflessly as possible, precisely how to preserve both the agelessness and the contemporaneity of every Shakespeare play.

To give some examples closer to home, I would like to mention how, in our stumbling way, we have been trying at Yale to investigate from time to time the problems of modern Shakespeare production, not to mention production of the classics as a whole. There we encourage our directing students, in addition to the new plays they do, to develop a classical production according to a concept that they find meaningful to the play and to themselves, and to expose this concept well in advance to argument and debate with their instructors and the rest of the class. The concept must then be realized, of course, through close coordination with designers and with actors; but whatever the outcome in actual production, the habit of finding a metaphor for a play that expresses something meaningful to all those concerned with it, as well as for the audiences, is being instilled in an early stage.

In our professional company, the Yale Repertory Theatre, this process is extended further, so that no production is ever chosen simply because an actor wants a choice role, but rather because the production as a whole will make some poetic statement to the audience. My own production of *Macbeth*, three years ago, for example, was an effort to adapt that play to a world conditioned by the space age and by such movies as *2001*—finding a new function for the three weird sisters, inspired by Banquo's line when he first encounters them: "What are these, so withered and so wild in their attire, that look not like the inhabitants of the earth, and yet are on it?" It was our contention in production that the witches were not the inhabitants of the earth, but visitors from another world, who had materialized in our midst at a primitive time in our history in order to change the line of succession in Scotland, and by that change to alter human history. This fanciful idea helped us find solutions to certain problems of the play—as, for example, the identity of the third murderer, who now became one of these space creatures in human form, saving Banquo's son from the other murderers so that he might accede to the throne at some future date. Similarly, we had Duncan come back on stage, after his murder, in the form of the Porter answering the knocking at the gate—resurrected by the weird creatures as a controlled thing to do their bidding. The masque of kings, which Macbeth is shown at the end, thus became a filmed montage of Banquo wearing the royal robes of eight different royal figures, from primitive times right down to the modern period—the visual realization of the aim of the creatures to alter Scottish and English history.

The reason for this grew not just out of my own passion for science fiction, but rather out of a conviction that *Macbeth* is about time, its passing, its inevitability, and its uncontrollability. We set the play in the most primitive period possible, when men wore skins and ate their meat raw, against a background very much like Stonehenge, with three huge dolmens as the spaceships on whose surface the creatures materialized in projections. The idea, borrowed from Von Daniken's *Chariots of the Gods* and Arthur Clarke's *Childhood's End*, was that primitive men were once visited by intelligent extraterrestrial creatures, who then vacated the earth after having worked their will on our forebears, leaving us with myths as memories of their visit—one of which was *Macbeth.*

Well, not much of this was clear in production—mostly for technical reasons; the idea was too complicated to be realized through our equipment, which has made me long, in weaker moments, for the kind of technology that Disney developed, say, in his Haunted House exhibit in Disney World, where three-dimensional transparent images are projected before your eyes, dancing, drinking, and carousing in a roomful of ghosts. But it is also my hindsight sense that if a concept needs a lot of technology to realize it, it is probably not appropriate for the necessary limitations of the stage.

This year, in a production of *The Tempest,* directed by Moni Yakim and Alvin Epstein, we tried to amalgamate the timelessness and contemporaneity of Shakespeare by grafting onto the original text the music that Purcell had written for his opera of the play some seventy years later. The music thus became an extension of Prospero's magic, as well as being very beautiful in itself, and the entire work took on the stately and statuesque qualities of a masque. Instead of one Ariel, we had seven, both male and female, led by the beautiful Carmen de Lavallade, dressed in an elastic gauze-like fabric that looked like mist swirling around Prospero's feet; this functioned as an imprisoning fabric for the graceful sprites, thus leaving them immobilized by their costumes, yet, because of their number, capable of being here, there, and everywhere at once. At the end, when Prospero sets Ariel free, Miss de Lavallade, high up on the stage, emerged naked from her costume, like a butterfly from its cocoon, as the orchestra played the lovely concluding strains of the opera.

In another vein, we are currently doing a version of *Hamlet* in our production of *Watergate Classics*—a satirical revue that attempts to turn the "no more masterpieces" idea to political purposes, demonstrating how such works as *Oedipus, Waiting for Godot, Krapp's Last Tape, Iphigenia in Aulis,* and others contain material that both prophesies and illuminates America's present Presidential dilemmas. This particular *Hamlet,* written by Jeremy Geidt and Jonathan Marks, and retitled *Samlet,* casts Sam Ervin in the part of the Prince, trying desperately to revenge himself on King Claudickus with a gavel; Haldeman and Ehrlichman as Rosencrantz and Guildenstern, continually being confused with one another; John Mitchell as the King's counselor, Felonius, giving larcenous advice to his protégé, John Dean, as Laertes; and a trio of players, including John Wayne, Sammy Davis, Jr., and Frank Sinatra, enacting "The Death of Spirago" in order to catch the conscience of the King. Meanwhile the ghost of Uncle Sam hovers on the ramparts, crying for revenge—and asking the audience, after the King has triumphed over his absent-minded adversary Samlet, to "remember me."

This, of course, is a revue sketch, which can hardly be put forward seriously as a production of *Hamlet*; but it never-theless embodies the idea that Shakespeare is a vast storehouse that can be raided for virtually any purpose—and somehow manage to survive. And I would like to close with the plea, in spite of my own strictures, that we try to develop more tolera-tion in regard to Shakespeare experimentation, even when it goes awry. I am not suggesting that we lower our standards, nor am I taking back my criticism of certain approaches to Shakespeare that I personally consider somewhat empty. Rather, I am proposing that we stop going to Shakespeare productions in the expectation of seeing something definitive, and treat these productions less as total re-creations of the works than as directorial essays on them. Changing Shakespeare is not the same thing as desecrating a painting, for though an artwork is permanently damaged by such treatment, a dramatic work continues to exist, regardless of what you do to it, because it still exists purely as a text. The theatre should be a place of dialogue, where each production of a play inspires enough excitement, even in opposition, to engender another production of that play in reply. And it is this continuing dialogue that keeps masterpieces alive on the stage, just as the dialogue among Shakespearean critics helps to keep the plays alive on the page.

In short, I would like to see an answer to Peter Brook's interpretation of *A Midsummer Night's Dream*—one, say, that rescued that play from acrobatics and returned it to romance.* Or I would like to see a reply to his *King Lear* that reminded us that this action took place within a thundering universe in which the protagonist was almost as mighty as the storm he was defying. This is not to speak in disparagement of these two fine productions, but rather out of respect for them; for it is as a stimulus to thought and feeling that productions have their true success, and not simply as objects of praise and veneration. I must say that what I miss most in American theatre today is a critical and audience atmosphere in which productions are interpreted for what they are trying to say, and judged on the basis of whether they say that effectively, rather than treated as objects either of excessive praise or excessive blame—hits or flops that add nothing to our experience except the capacity to say we have been present at a play. But this atmosphere, in which critics and audiences discuss productions rather than simply trade opinions, is perhaps the same kind of atmosphere in which such provocative productions are formulated. For it is in the context of such theatrical intelligence and imagination, rare as it is, that Shakespeare shows us he is not just for an age, but for all time. (1974)

* Alvin Epstein directed such a production, a year later, at the Yale Repertory Theatre in the spring of 1975.

A Dean's Goodbye

A Speech to the Graduates of the School of Drama

Graduation at the Drama School is traditionally both a joyful and a melancholy time, but it seems a little more melancholy to me this year than usual, because I am saying goodbye to a particularly spirited, talented, and good-natured class. I feel melancholy, too, because I have had the opportunity to know this class, owing to my own leave in England, only two out of the customary three years. I feel a little cheated of your company, in other words, and would like to enjoy it a little longer—a thought that probably chills the marrow of those who feel they have been here half their lives already.

Checking the list of graduates this year, I see the names of good friends, gifted associates, and fine artists and scholars. The Yale School of Drama has great pride in the sons and daughters it has graduated, but I don't know when a single graduating class, taken as an aggregate, has been able to boast, in virtually every division, such a combination of talent and character: inventive and original designers, conscientious technical craftsmen, daring and audacious playwrights, versatile transforming actors, patient and efficient administrators, careful and knowledgeable directors; even the critics seem more generous and free of malice. The third-year acting-directing class, third-year designers and technicians, and third-year administrators, with whom the Yale Repertory Theatre has had the privilege to collaborate this year, have helped to bring the Rep to some kind of artistic culmination that will always make this season memorable in my mind; and the playwrights and directors in this class have brought genuine distinction to the school projects, one of which (*The Idiots Karamazov*) will be produced during next year's professional season.

So I'm very happy for you on this day, and take leave of you with less than my usual worry about your artistic futures. At the Gala the other night, one student sang a little song to the effect that you have an MFA, a DFA, a CERT, but you don't have a J-O-B: that song speaks the despair of the profession to which we belong. The extraordinary thing, these days, is that most of the people who leave here do find J-O-Bs in the theatre, and many of you already have yours. I don't have much fear that the professional theatre world will long remain ignorant of what you have to offer, and that even in this depressed profession, good jobs will eventually be found for all. I wish the financial condition of the Rep was sound enough for us to extend job opportunities to every graduating student who deserves or wants them. But this is clearly impossible, and probably even undesirable, since most of you should be encouraged to breathe other kinds of air than the hectic, controversial, thick, and sometimes stifling atmosphere of New Haven.

In short, I don't worry that most of you will find some kind of employment in the theatre. My real worry, which I'm sure you share, is over the quality of the employment you'll find, and how that will affect your expectations and your hopes. There is a line in one of Shakespeare's sonnets in which he speaks of "the expense of spirit in a waste of shame." So much theatre in America today is a waste and a shame that you will undoubtedly find yourself worrying from time to time about the expenditure of your spirit. All of you have been trained to be technically expert in your particular discipline, which is why you will soon find yourselves in demand by the theatre; but I hope something else has been going on around here over the past three years besides technical expertise, which will keep you always sensitive to how your spirit is being expended, and ever wary as to whether you are involved in what constitutes a waste of shame.

The Yale School of Drama, despite its emphasis on the techniques of the theatre, is not designed to be a vocational school, offering various courses in job training, any more than the Yale Repertory Theatre is designed to provide mere entertainment for its audiences. Something else should be going on here—something more hortatory, more visionary, more demanding, less utilitarian—and that something can only be described in embarrassing moral and even religious terms, as a form of spiritual indoctrination designed to help bring about the beginning of a soul in the American theatre. It's not anything we have talked about half as much as I would have liked; and I'm not even certain that all the faculty would agree that this should be our function or our purpose. But I do know that this is what obsesses me most of my waking days, what keeps me here, and what will ultimately constitute my sense of whether the school has succeeded or failed in what I regard as its primary purpose.

For this place is measured only by two criteria: the works of art it is able to produce, and the kind of people it manages to develop. The first measure is chancy and ephemeral. Most productions in the theatre, no matter how ambitious or sincere, are disappointing, just like most work in the novel, poetry, painting, or music. The most we can hope for there is that their intentions will be correct, that they will be designed out of artistic motives, rather than commercial, power, or fame drives, and that even when they fail, the failure will be honorable. This, of course, is an impossible demand to place on any theatre, given the exigencies and tribulations of support in a country that is still essentially philistine; but regardless of occasional mistakes, and more than occasional failures, the quality that animates a theatre is its continuing vision and goals, and the fact that it keeps its direction in spite of occasional detours.

And even in that rarest of moments when a theatre breaks through out of its groping and probing and manages to create a work of art, that work is written on water, since it has life, after the conclusion of its run, only in the minds and memories of those who have seen it with the proper response. The very spontaneity of the theatre, its life of the moment, which it possesses in contradistinction to all the written arts, is the source of its limitations, since there is no way to hold that moment, fixed and immutable, as a permanent testament of achievement.

So the soul of a theatre rests not in any single one of its

productions, successful or not, but rather in its vision and continuity, and this can only be built by the people associated with it. A former student at the school returned, a few days ago, from a distinguished theatre in the West where he was holding a good position, and told me that he was enjoying his work and felt proud to be associated with such a respected organization. But underneath his pleasure and sense of achievement, he felt a nagging worry, and that was that despite the prominence of his theatre and its national reputation, it lacked this very soul I have been talking about; it seemed to have no purpose other than to survive.

I knew when I spoke to him, however, that his theatre now had a better chance to develop such a soul, because of his association with it. And I knew, too, from his conversation that the school had had that impact on him that I dreamed about, that if every graduating class produced just one individual like this, then American theatre had a chance not just to survive but to flourish and grow. I began to understand, too, that the ephemeral theatre found its permanence and immutability in just such people who were willing to commit themselves to an institution and help to improve it. This didn't mean exploiting the institution for one's fame and advancement; it didn't mean subordinating oneself like a servile and sheepish creature to whatever shameful ends the institution asked you to serve; it didn't mean insubordination either, pulling out on the sidelines and criticizing from a safe, opinionated distance, or malcontentedly refusing to do work that didn't suit your own immediate needs or standards. No, it meant throwing yourself into the work of an institution with all the passion and devotion and craft at your control, and loving the ideal of the work so much that you kept pressing the institution to express its goals, and pressing it to try to realize them.

So the future theatre of America, if America is going to have theatres in the future, will be constituted not only of what you are able to create as highly trained professionals, but of what you are able to provide them with as highly motivated visionaries. You are entering a theatre situation, as far as the permanent institutions are concerned, where money is becoming more and more of a problem, where slowly increasing government support is being canceled out by quickly increasing withdrawal of capricious private foundations, and where financial managers will probably begin to replace artistic directors as the arbiters of theatrical destiny. This means that more and more decisions will be based on economic necessity, and that pressures will continually mount to attract large audiences with safe and conventional fare rather than to take risks with the untried in an attempt to advance the boundaries of the art. Even at this moment, Broadway producers, who preside over a moribund situation, are trying to amalgamate with resident theatres, which at least retain some vitality; and such a union, whatever its doubtful prospects for the commercial theatre, cannot help but rob the non-profit resident theatre of what is left of its soul.

In such circumstances, your function is going to be crucial. Naturally, the first need, especially of those with families, will be to hold a job and survive. But there are ways also to hold your jobs without letting your institution bargain away its birthright. I assume you believe in your profession, because you chose it, because you devoted at least three difficult years to training in it, and because you are now preparing to enter it. This country is trembling on the edge of something, and only you can determine which way it will fall. The agony of Watergate has exposed a rot not only in the highest reaches of government, but in almost every area of American life. You can either join that corruption, ignore it, withdraw from it, or try to reform it; and whether you are prepared to be a moral force in the theatre, which in part reflects that corruption, will have a profound effect on the kind of world we are all going to share after your graduation. Your spirits must not be expendable in a waste of shame; but you can help define the proper conditions for your spirit, and for the spirit of the time.

Good luck and happiness attend you.   (1974)

Broadway and the Nonprofit Theatre: A Misalliance

One of the issues raised at the First Annual Congress of Theatre (FACT), held on the Princeton campus last June—it is perhaps the central question facing the American theatre at the present time—was whether the ailing Broadway theatre might find some measure of financial and artistic relief through an alliance with the nonprofit theatre movement. Could the old lion lie down with the young lamb? Was it conceivable that these two mutually suspicious, competing, and opposing systems could establish a fruitful liaison, despite their traditional differences? It was certainly obvious from the flirtatious manner in which nonprofit theatre representatives were being treated at this conference, most conspicuously by representatives of the League of Broadway Theatres, that they were being courted for romantic purposes, and if marriage wasn't being considered, then some sort of tentative common-law relationship was about to be proposed.

For the first time, Broadway seemed to be dropping its defensive booster attitudes and conceding some doubts about survival. Indeed, the greatest stir of the conference was caused when Bernard Jacobs, executive director of the Shubert organization, complained rather wistfully, "There's no future for profit theatre as I know it." Implicit in that remark, however, was not so much a loss of faith in the Broadway system as a determination to reconstitute that system along more viable lines; and one clear signpost pointed in the direction of the relatively healthy and vital nonprofit theatre—a compound of resident companies, off-off-Broadway, and permanent producing institutions.

As a matter of fact, a channel between the two systems was already being dug before the conference began. As Mel Gussow observed in a recent article on the subject in the *Times,* twenty-one of the forty-six shows that opened on Broadway last year were first presented in nonprofit theatres, the most profitable being the Broadway productions of *Candide* and *Raisin,* which originated, respectively, at the Chelsea Theatre in Brooklyn and the Arena Stage in Washington. Increasingly over the past five years, the nonprofit theatres have been transferring their most successful productions, fully cast, to Broadway under commercial sponsorship, and although the results have ranged from financial successes such as the Public Theatre's *That Championship Season* and *Two Gentlemen of Verona* to such financial disappointments as the Long Wharf's *The Changing Room* and *Solitaire/Double Solitaire,* the economic risks of such moves have proved considerably lower than the odds-crazy gamble of conventional Broadway investment in untried plays or musicals.

The advantages of such an alliance to the Broadway system are perfectly obvious. The current scarcity of money, combined with the unpredictability of Times Square taste, makes it essential for Broadway produc ers to reduce their risks, and the nonprofit movement represents a rich source of wholly subsidized out-of-town tryouts. The *Times* reports that a large number of these producers have, as a result, begun to scout the resident, university, and off-off-Broadway theatres for products that might be cheaply moved to a Broadway house; and even some of the most successful people in the commercial theatre—Neil Simon being the most recent example—are preparing to let their Broadway-bound plays be produced first in nonprofit resident theatres.

The advantages to the nonprofit system are also perfectly obvious. At a time when subsidies are in short supply and every artistic director is scratching to cover his deficit, a commercial New York run for a resident theatre production promises considerable box-office income and royalties, besides enhancing the theatre's local reputation with its regional audience and creating the media visibility now required to attract foundation grants.

It all sounds like a splendid practical solution to the problems of both these troubled systems, and already hands are being extended over the relationship in happy benediction. But, feeling a little like the churlish guest who interrupts the ceremony to say why the partners should not be joined, I am compelled now to speak or forever hold my peace: the relationship is potentially adulterous, the offspring may prove monstrous, and the institutional theatre is in danger of losing whatever chastity it still possesses.

Let me try to explain this ungracious outburst.

The nonprofit theatre was originally conceived—much like the repertory theatre in England—as an alternative to the commercial system, not as a replacement for it. In its purest manifestation, it was to be devoted to serious theatre, not entertainment, its purpose to generate works of art rather than multiply profits or advance careers. In the United States, the idea of the nonprofit theatre was to establish decentralized permanent centers sufficiently distant from the hit-happy pressures of Broadway where a community of artists with common goals might develop organically related programs of plays instead of random one-shot gold strikes.

The advances of this young movement have not been accomplished without difficulty, for the distractions of vanity, careerism, profit, glamour, and fame are still the major snares of the American theatre. But nothing so endangers the soul of the nonprofit theatre—not the loss of its actors to TV or the movies, not the preference of its audiences for more conventional fare, not its shortage of money—as its present tendency to service Broadway with potentially marketable products. Why should this be when English companies—notably the National Theatre, the Royal Shakespeare Company, and the Bristol Old Vic—have been known to transfer productions to the West End with no apparent loss of artistic integrity? The answer is related to the reason why the English repertory movement has such a long, secure history and ours such a precarious and short one. English companies are sufficiently established in the culture, sufficiently subsidized by the Arts Council, and sufficiently large in their complement of actors to maintain an identity despite occasional commercial ventures, whereas the embryonic American theatres have as yet neither the resources, the internal cohesion, the confidence, the sense of purpose, nor the cultural support to resist being absorbed by an opposing system of values.

The danger of a liaison with the commercial theatre is less obvious in the case of such nonprofit producing units as the New York Public Theatre and the Mark Taper Forum in Los Angeles, though the threat to their founding principles may well be potentially greater. Since these theatres are devoted to developing sequential productions with separate casts, there would seem to be little disruption involved in moving a play that has found favor with its own audience to a larger Broadway theatre for an extended run—especially when the theatre continues to produce its other work in the meanwhile. Still, a theatre that has benefited from this kind of move may be tempted, intentionally or not, to choose its future programs on the basis of what might be successful in the commercial theatre, and gradually, subtly, perhaps even unconsciously, it may one day find itself engaged in a subsidized form of Broadway producing. It is one thing to reduce the element of financial risk; it is quite another to reduce the element of artistic risk, for this is the principle on which the best nonprofit American theatres are founded. When an institutional theatre begins mounting vehicles for stars or producing light entertainments of a kind appropriate to Broadway, then it has effectively identified with the commercial system in everything but the structure of its finances.

The danger to a resident theatre with a permanent company is even more serious, since a continuing relationship with the commercial theatre could become a threat to its very existence. When a fully cast production is transferred from its regional base to an open-ended run in New York, the whole process of company work is being violated. (I speak not of situations where that process can be preserved, such as tours, brief residencies, and limited engagements, or of New York engagements with replacement casts.) Considering the limited size of most American companies, a move of this kind leaves the home theatre with a severely reduced complement of disgruntled actors or with a pickup cast for its subsequent productions; it freezes the performer in a single role instead of letting him stretch through a variety of parts; it implies that the theatre's subscription audience is made up of second-class citizens; and it may even have a deleterious effect on company morale, since it shakes the confidence of the more committed members in the resolution and seriousness of the directorship. To transfer the most successful production of the season to Broadway is to imply that the idea of decentralization is a hypocrisy and that we are still in the world of the Big Break; it is to concede the common Broadway assumption that an actor is not really "professional" until he appears on the commercial stage. Worst of all, a move of this kind introduces into the usually deliberate, humane, and relaxed process of resident theatre work all those overheated anxieties and feverish panics that traditionally characterize the Broadway stage.

I speak from experience, not from a self-righteous distance, so let me try to document my last remark with some personal history concerning the Yale Repertory Theatre. And although this describes a situation in which Broadway came to us rather than we to Broadway, it dramatizes the problems afflicting such marriages in whatever house they inhabit.

When I was in London last year, I happened to meet with Burt Shevelove, who, thirty years previously as a student at the Yale School of Drama, had staged a memorable production of Aristophanes' *The Frogs* in the Payne-Whitney swimming pool. The occasion seemed to me so unique, and the idea so wacky, that I invited Burt to do the production again, this time with the professional company of the Yale Repertory Theatre. He generously agreed, and we both looked forward to a delightful lark.

Neither of us had plans for the show beyond its one-week run: the Yale pool is hardly portable. For Burt, the invitation had nostalgic interest as an opportunity to work in some old haunts; for us, it had financial possibilities as a post-season benefit for a theatre always in need of money, as well as artistic value as a collaboration with the gifted co-author of *A Funny Thing Happened on the Way to the Forum*. I reasoned that Burt had already proved his ability to adapt classical Roman comedy to the techniques of vaudeville and burlesque; now I was eager to see him handle a similar challenge with classical Greek comedy.

Before long, Burt announced to me, with considerable enthusiasm, that he had managed to enlist the aid of Stephen Sondheim as composer and lyricist for the show, and while this seemed to change the nature of the enterprise somewhat, stepping outside the bounds of a Yale-Shevelove reunion and tilting the work toward musical comedy, I raised no objection to this or his subsequent production demands. But it was soon relatively clear that our resources were not always going to prove acceptable either to Sondheim or to Shevelove. Sondheim insisted on bringing in his own orchestrator and his own musical director, while Burt was eager to cast outside of the company, with Larry Blyden in the central role of Dionysus.

Similarly, the modest cast we had discussed in London was growing to enormous proportions, including not only our resident professional company of 18 but also a singing and dancing chorus of 28, a swimming chorus of 18, and an orchestra of 12, not to mention a backstage contingent of 35. With over 100 people involved in the enterprise, the production had blossomed into a spectacular extravaganza, completely beyond our control. And since the full script was not ready until the day of the opening, and the full score until after the opening, the four-week rehearsal period concluded with three or four days of intensive, exhausting overtime drill sessions.

Working with Shevelove, Sondheim, Blyden, and their associates was always rewarding and nearly always good-humored, but it was soon pretty obvious that the Yale Repertory Theatre was expected to function less as a collaborator than as a servicing unit. In this unaccustomed role, it was not to prove entirely satisfactory. Burt continued to go about his business indefatigably under difficult conditions, but as the opening approached, it grew more and more clear that the system under which he was used to working was in serious conflict with our own procedures. He expected to rehearse the actors, Broadway-style, for twelve hours a day on the final week and twenty-four hours on the day before opening, whereas the resident theatre contract stipulates eight-hour days and an obligatory day off; he wanted to replace two actors he was dissatisfied with, whereas our unwritten code forbids firing permanent people from a single show; he was aiming to complete production by the time of the press opening on Tuesday night, whereas we considered the audience on Monday night (our official opening) to be just as deserving of a finished production as the critics. The Broadway people found our manner of work to be haphazardly unprofessional in their sense of the term, while we were surprised by all the last-minute pressure being imposed on a single production—and one intended as a holiday at that—after a season of seven regular plays.

I suppose the most disturbing thing to me personally was the kind of atmosphere *The Frogs* introduced into our world. On the Tuesday press opening, a busload of notables was shipped up from New York City, creating serious hassles over the unreserved seats and a lot of kissing backstage, while the largest group of reviewers ever to visit a Yale production descended on the pool. The opening, in short, was indistinguishable from a glittering Broadway occasion, and, partly as a result, the Tuesday performance was a mess, with many of the actors forcing and one forgetting the lines of a new speech he had been handed just a few hours before.

The audience and press response was generally enthusiastic, and the show had many brilliant moments, particularly the sensational first appearance of the swimming chorus of frogs to the accompaniment of Sondheim's rousing music. But not many in our professional company looked back upon it as a happy experience, and a few thought it shook us to our foundations. The technical crew resented the way it was used, some of the actors felt manipulated and unfulfilled, while our management spent most of its time engaged in efforts at melioration. Those who say I should have known better are undoubtedly right (my instinct to place the show after our regular season suggests I knew it would not be representative of our work) and whatever blame there is belongs entirely to me. Even the expected financial benefits failed to materialize. Despite the fact that virtually every seat in the 1,700-seat gymnasium-pool was sold during the run, the expenses of the production grew so large that the budget came in at $18,000 over its initial $25,000 estimate, and all we were able to realize was a $7,000 profit. It was a signal demonstration of how even the "hits" of the Broadway theatre can sometimes prove to be Pyrrhic victories.

Anyone concerned over the survival of a pluralistic culture is concerned over the survival of any aspect of that culture, and I would consider it a serious blow to the American stage should the commercial theatre collapse. But there must be a way to save it without compromising the nonprofit theatre as well. Those of us in the nonprofit theatre movement have watched with considerable anguish as many of our actors, directors, playwrights, and designers have bartered their talents in sterile undertakings. Must we now barter our theatres as well? The strength of the nonprofit theatre is growing. It can be measured by the desperate way in which Broadway, drowning, tries to pull itself to safety by holding on to its shoulders. Let those of us who work in these theatres take care not to be pulled down under as well. (1974)

Seminal and Consumer Theatre

I should like to propose two categories that would define the theatre institutions currently operating in the United States. This definition will not be based on geographical, economic, or structural principles but is inspired rather by artistic goals and practices—a yardstick that seems to me eminently more interesting than where a theatre is located or what constitutes its chief source of funds. The categories I propose are "seminal theatre" and "consumer theatre." Before defining these terms, however, let me explain why I find the current distinctions somewhat inadequate, in view of recent developments in the American theatre.

It is still common shorthand to distinguish between two

distinct types of theatre systems in this country. "Broadway," as personified by individual producers working in hope of profit on a show-by-show basis, and "regional" or "nonprofit" theatre, as exemplified by partially subsidized permanent institutions located throughout the length and breadth of the land. These categories are valuable enough in suggesting the differences between the commercial and noncommercial structures in regard to their finances, but they are too broad to do justice to the full range of contemporary theatre in America. Worse, they are philosophically and even geographically misleading. Just as the generic term "Broadway" designates a form of commercial producing that is hardly limited to one street in New York, so the word "regional" (when used as a synonym for the nonprofit system) evokes overtones of provincialism that are inappropriate to the sophistication of this movement, not to mention its vitality in various urban centers, including New York.

It is true that the modern repertory movement grew out of an impulse to decentralize the American theatre, with the Guthrie Theatre settling in Minneapolis, the Association of Producing Artists (APA) at the University of Michigan, and the American Conservatory Theatre (after brief sojourns in Pittsburgh and Chicago) in San Francisco. But while decentralization was important to the purposes of this movement at its inception, it was at no point a "regional" development in the sense of being indigenous to a special province or place. Tyrone Guthrie chose Minneapolis, and rejected Boston, for the site of his new theatre, not because he had any special affinity with the traditions of Minnesota but because he wanted to be distant enough to escape the pulls and pressures he saw threatening embryonic permanent companies. And the APA company was sufficiently cosmopolitan in the range of its repertory to take up residence, after its Michigan seasons and several seasons of tours, in Broadway's Lyceum Theatre— where it expired a few years later from some of the afflictions Guthrie had diagnosed.

Similarly, while New York City was relatively laggard in this movement, considering its size and former pre-eminence as a theatrical center, it now supports a large number of nonprofit institutions, ranging from the showcase Lincoln Center operation to the experimental Café La Mama. The city still has difficulty in maintaining a first-rate permanent company because of all the pieces that get chewed out of it by star-hungry agents and producers, but theatres with permanent staffs of one kind or another have proliferated in the past few years until they now dominate the theatrical life of the city, at the same time that commercial theatre activity has been declining.

If the old distinction between Broadway and regional theatre is not proving useful for geographical reasons, the alternative distinction between Broadway and nonprofit theatre has also begun to lose its meaning, primarily because the latter is composed of so many divisions and subdivisions that it is futile to include them under a single heading. If I may mention a few of these, we have permanent companies (the American Conservatory Theatre in San Francisco) as opposed to operations that have separate casts during the same season (the Mark Taper Forum in Los Angeles); repertory companies (the Guthrie) as opposed to producing organizations that present several plays simultaneously (the New York Public Theatre); experimental producing units (the Chelsea Theatre Center at the Brooklyn Academy of Music) as opposed to conventional producing units (off-Broadway's Circle in the Square); classical repertories (the City Center Acting Company in New York City) as opposed to new play repertories (the Circle Repertory Theatre Company in New York City); classical companies devoted to Shakespeare (the American Shakespeare Festival Theatre in Stratford, Connecticut) as opposed to those reviving a broad range of dramatic literature (New York's Phoenix Theatre); companies that rotate as many as three plays a week (the Yale Repertory Theatre) as opposed to those that perform sequentially one play after another (the Long Wharf in New Haven); multiple-play companies (the Arena Stage in Washington, D.C.) as opposed to single-project groups (the Manhattan Project); poetic performing groups (off-Broadway's Open Theatre) as opposed to political performing groups (off-Broadway's Living Theatre); black theatre and Chicano theatre (the Negro Ensemble Company in New York City, and El Teatro Campesino in southern California) as opposed to camp theatre (off-Broadway's Ridiculous Theatrical Company). Obviously, the categories are as numerous as the theatre companies themselves, and they intersect and separate at so many points that discriminations become difficult and confusing.

At the risk of compounding the confusion even further, let me now define my own suggested categories: seminal theatre, by which I mean an institution that develops new playwrights, new techniques, and new approaches to classical material; and consumer theatre, by which I mean an institution that adheres fairly closely to the standard repertory and the more conventional new plays. As their names suggest, seminal theatre attempts to sow fresh seeds with the hope that they might eventually flower in the general consciousness of the time, while consumer theatre is content to satisfy its immediate audiences, who absorb the theatrical product in the same spirit as they would digest a good meal.

Put another way, consumer theatre is directed toward the public, seminal theatre toward the material; the one is community-oriented, the other has national ambitions; the one sits comfortably within its environment, the other is subject to controversy and unpopularity; the one measures its success by the box office, the other by its impact on theatre history. Obviously, consumer theatre has taken over, nationally, many of the cultural and entertainment services that used to be provided by Broadway, whereas seminal theatre has appropriated the laboratory functions associated with the early off-Broadway movement.

It is a measure of the difference between these two kinds of institutions that while the seminal theatre's program is too varied and idiosyncratic to be summarized, the consumer theatre's program is fairly predictable. At its least ambitious, it would serve up the desserts of the dinner-theatre menu, such as revivals of successful musicals and staple comedies like those of Neil Simon; at its most ambitious, it would offer the *haute cuisine* of classical and modern plays. Shakespeare's better-known works would certainly be central to the repertory, produced either in doublet and hose or in some novel external setting that simply changes the time and place of a play. (You may recognize the American Shakespeare Festival at Stratford as perhaps the prime example of consumer theatre in classical robes.) Other classical plays produced by consumer theatre might include a Molière comedy (usually *Tartuffe* or *The Misanthrope*), possibly a Greek tragedy and, inevitably, the durable *Cyrano de Bergerac,* perhaps with a popular movie star making a temporary return to the stage in the title role.

Among modern classics, Ibsen's *A Doll's House* and *Ghosts* would have their place; all of Chekhov's mature plays; Brecht's *Threepenny Opera*; O'Neill's later works; the more popular plays of Williams and Miller; a vintage American farce like *The Front Page* or *You Can't Take It with You*; Synge's *Playboy of the Western World* and O'Casey's *Juno and the Paycock*; and, of course, Thornton Wilder's pastoral American myth, *Our Town.* Whatever new plays were attempted would conform pretty closely to the pattern of the modern works already in the repertory, being realistic-psychological plays of character, generally about family life, possibly with a little social comment, and either contributed by established American playwrights or imported from London after they had already proved their popularity with audiences.

Now what could be wrong with this? At worst, it's harmless; at best, it represents a sensible, healthy helping of culture, even though the spectator is seeing a good many plays with which he, as an educated member of the middle class, is already acquainted. Such a program contains little that is cheap or spurious; many of the plays are among the greatest in literature; the productions are usually competent and sometimes even distinguished; and the offerings are guaranteed to keep both actors and spectators satisfied. This kind of theatre is the sort of institution that any community would be proud to support, through either the box office, subscription, or private contribution—it is the theatrical equivalent of a season ticket to the local opera (or the Metropolitan Opera Company) and a membership in the local museum (or the Metropolitan Museum of Art). To have such a theatre in the community is to possess a valuable cultural asset, which, like the museum and the opera, keeps the standard works continually in the minds of the public.

And what about seminal theatre? Can this be called a cultural asset? Continuously experimenting at the expense of the audience, maddening in its process of trial and error, it is either mangling and mutilating beloved classics, like a child pulling apart a precious heirloom to examine its works (say, the Performance Group's *Dionysus in '69*), or fabricating strange hallucinations in which people just don't behave like normal human beings (say, the Open Theatre's *Mutation Show*). Too often, such experiments seem like an end in themselves, where the spectator is asked to sit still while the actors go through their preparation exercises; too often, the success of the venture seems to be measured by how deeply the audience has been offended. By now I am sure that just about everybody has had enough of those naked love gropes, those steamy bodies clasping each other in an ecstasy of passionless narcissism, those shouting matches and glowering abuses, those arrogant attitudes in regard to everything previously created. Admittedly, the radical avant-garde has lately given seminal theatre a black eye, making it seem not high-spirited but rather juvenile, not adventurous but rather exhibitionistic, not proud but rather hostile and aggressive.

Still, whatever its failings, the idea of seminal theatre remains, to my mind, one of the most necessary conceptions in the performing arts, for without that idea there would be no hope of theatrical breakthrough and advance. We should remember that there would be no vital consumer theatre, whatever its popularity, without seminal theatre, whatever its minority status, just as the museum and the opera would soon become empty repositories of the past without the artist's studio and the opera workshop. It was seminal theatre that first took the risks on the current staples of consumer theatre: Ibsen at Antoine's Théâtre Libre; Brecht at the Berliner Ensemble; Chekhov at the Moscow Art Theatre; O'Neill at the Provincetown Playhouse; Synge and O'Casey at the Abbey Theatre; most of the English writers at the Royal Court; Williams and Miller on Broadway, when Broadway still had seminal ambitions. Even Shakespeare's and Molière's original companies were seminal theatres in the sense that they were committed largely to untried works, whereas the latter-day Old Vic and Comédie Française began to atrophy once they ceased to originate new plays or production techniques. In short, what consumer theatre successfully markets are the fruits of seminal theatre when they have become ripe enough for mass consumption.

It is, moreover, seminal theatre that has developed most of the significant new talents of the American stage—Sam Shepard, Jean-Claude van Itallie, and David Rabe among playwrights; André Gregory, Robert Wilson, Joseph Chaikin, and Richard Foreman among ensemble directors; Joseph Papp, Robert Kalfin, and Ellen Stewart among artistic directors, to name a few—just as, somewhat less recently, it was responsible for the Shakespeare reinterpretations of Peter Brook with the Royal Shakespeare Company, the improvisational methods of Paul Sills at the Second City, and the monastic chimeras of Jerzy Grotowski with his Polish Laboratory Theatre. At worst, it is a theatre infatuated with novelty and fads, and therefore easily assimilated into commercial entertainment; at best, it speaks directly to the current fears, apprehensions, and anxieties of a culture (rather than its desires or fantasies), staking a claim on the outer borders of our consciousness.

Both these theatres, therefore, deserve the support and encouragement of society, the one for preserving our traditions, the other for subjecting these traditions to scrutiny and revision. But lest I complete this analysis in an uncharacteristic mood of tolerance, let me try to say why I personally find consumer theatre often tepid and lifeless, and cast my lot with its erratic rival.

If the prime virtue of the stage is to surprise and its prime failing is to bore, consumer theatre is defective in that it rarely tells us anything we don't already know. To see another actor warbling Hamlet's soliloquies or gasping over Cyrano's white plume, to watch Wilder's Stage Manager snapping his suspenders again or Stanley Kowalski breaking another plate, to find myself in one more kitchen or locker room agonizing over the domestic problems of small contemporary figures, is to convert me instantly into an inert mass, eying the exit when I'm not checking my watch. This, admittedly, may be a personal problem, and I have been told more than once that I have seen too many plays to cast a less than jaded eye on the general run of production. My critics argue that most people, and especially the young, may be seeing these plays for the first time, and are therefore likely to find something fresh and vigorous in even the most conventional productions.

I can only reply that audiences at consumer theatre (where I see very few people below middle age) often look as inert as I feel, despite their generous applause at the conclusion of the performance. And if I am jaundiced toward the common run of, say, Shakespearean production, then my experience as a youth suggests that I was born that way. Like many others, I was introduced to Shakespeare by the Margaret Webster-Maurice Evans productions then in vogue, with their stiff, declamatory, brocaded style of presentation—those productions almost turned me off Shakespeare for life. It wasn't until the Laurence Olivier film of *Henry V*—a minor play in a brilliant production—that I realized Shakespeare was a great poet and not a librettist for operatic singsong. As a result, I saw the movie twenty-seven times and developed a ravenous hunger for reading the plays. What Olivier did was a seminal act at the time, though it may not seem unusual today. He brought a naturalness and humanity to what before had seemed to me unmediated bombast; he found a fresh and original path to the heart of the play.

And that is what seminal theatre is destined to do—evoke the unusual at the heart of the known. Brecht had something like this in mind when he said that theatre should make the familiar strange and the strange familiar, awakening the dreams that lie dormant beneath the surface of everyday life. Consumer theatre, on the other hand, is already familiar in its classical form and humdrum in its modern expression—which is to say, it derives its strength and popularity from confirming the spectator in his theatregoing expectations. The other—risky, restless, irritating, short-lived—makes, in my opinion, the greater contribution to the life of the imagination, the greater claim on our bottomless capacity for surprise. (1974)

The Money Crisis and the Performing Arts

Funding for the performing arts—a relatively arcane subject that usually doesn't interest anyone except us poor beggars who have to rattle the tin cup—is now threatening to become a topic of national debate as a result of a report recently issued by the Ford Foundation. The report, which was four years in the making and cost $500,000 to produce, is titled "The Finances of the Arts." What this weighty, massive, 446-page document manages to say—by means of analyzing questionnaires, graphs, statistics, computer analysis, sociological data, and other such entertaining devices—is that if you think the performing arts are in financial trouble now, just wait until 1981. Assuming even the most optimistic upturn in the economy, the "earnings gap" (the foundation's current euphemism for "deficit") is expected to increase threefold in the next seven years, and the increase is more likely to be almost sixfold when all the inflationary effects are taken into account.

The Ford report concludes its narrative section with the warning that "if the arts are to remain healthy and to make the contribution to the conditions of human existence they are capable of, they will require increasing support from public funds, from corporations and, above all, from the private sector, particularly private patrons." Conspicuously missing from this list of sponsors are the private foundations, traditionally one of the most important sources of funding for the performing arts. And the Ford report hints that its own foundation will not only be unable to increase its support in the future but will probably be cutting back soon because of the impact of inflation on its portfolio. (The Rockefeller Foundation, second to Ford in this area, has already cut its arts budget almost in half, according to its Arts Director, Howard Klein, in response to a reordering of priorities by its new president, John Knowles.) Thus the Ford Foundation has spent half a million—a sum equal to the total annual budget of a modest resident theatre—to announce that the only hope for the future lies with the National Endowment for the Arts, the city and state cultural councils, the business community, and the "private sector"; namely, you, me, and our various wealthy relatives and friends.

Well, I don't know about you, but I am not in very good shape these days to make charitable contributions to the performing arts in addition to the price I pay for theatre, opera, symphony, ballet, and dance tickets, and I have an ominous feeling that the problem is widely shared—that if the arts had to depend on the voluntary largesse of private patrons, they would soon be extinct. This feeling was recently confirmed by a somewhat less expensive analysis that we at Yale conducted through an appeal inserted in one of our Repertory Theatre programs asking for tax-free contributions to help keep our theatre afloat: we received from a (very enthusiastic) audience of more than ten thousand exactly $33.50. What this may suggest—and what the Ford report fails to consider—is that inflation is presently hitting the individual pocketbook so hard that the private sector is no longer able to afford many donations to the performing arts, if indeed it can still afford the price of a subscription ticket.

So, if the private sector is not likely to prove a very dependable fount of money for the performing arts, what about the other sources mentioned in the Ford report? Certainly the business community represents a great reservoir of support in this area, but so far, that reservoir remains relatively untapped. A number of committed businessmen have been trying to open the sluices through councils, committees, conferences, and exhortations, and smaller corporations often make contributions to the local dance company or symphony. Still, grants of this kind are usually minimal, designed more as token civic gestures than as genuine support. A larger contribution is made by the national corporations (corporate giving almost trebled between 1965 and 1970), and institutions like Xerox, Exxon, and IBM have been underwriting many expensive television programs that feature theatre, music, and dance. Unfortunately, much of this seems to be an alternative form of commercial sponsorship in which the corporation moves its product through an appearance of public-spiritedness rather than hard sell—and it doesn't do much, if anything, for the performing arts organization outside of providing it with exposure and a small royalty from the television appearance. There are a number of exceptions to this generalization (one that I know of personally is the CBS Foundation's altruistic grant to Yale for support of playwrights and production of their new plays), but on the whole the business community has yet to regard the performing arts as valuable in themselves and not just a dignified vehicle for institutional advertising. I would be surprised, though delighted, to find this policy changing in future.

What about the government? Admittedly, federal funds for the arts have been expanding over the past ten years, and, contrary to the fears of those who thought the National Endowment for the Arts would be philistine in its posture and political in its control, this agency now constitutes the most enlightened, as well as the most generous, source of support in the country. Under the leadership of Nancy Hanks, appropriations for the arts have grown from $2.5 million in fiscal 1965 to $72 million in fiscal 1975, and there is every reason to hope that if the increase continues at its present rate, the contribution of the United States to the performing arts may soon be equal to that of the city of Vienna. Obviously, the National Endowment, despite its great strides and its promise of hope for the future, is still far from matching the record of the arts councils in England and Europe (for example, West Germany's support for the theatre alone amounts to $35 million annually); at the present time, the U.S. contributes less to the arts per capita than any other major country, including Canada.

The plain fact is that the National Endowment's rapid acceleration is not overcoming its late start, while Congressional resistance grows stronger as the annual appropriation approaches the $100 million mark. (This year, the Endowment's request was sliced by $8 million.) President Ford's determination to combat inflation by cutting down on government spending is not a happy omen for performing artists, either, who are still considered by many lawmakers to be effete and extravagant threats to a balanced budget. (Iowa's Republican Congressman H. R. Gross, in trying to cut the arts budget even further last July, referred to these artists as "little Twinkle Toes and those promoting lessons in belly dancing," which is an improvement, I suppose, on Richard Nixon's characterization of them as "Jews and left-wingers.")

Moreover, the arts appropriation is presently spread over so many areas that it manages to feed virtually everybody without filling anyone's stomach; those institutions operating outside of New York (which has the most generous state council in the country) are still fighting for existence, dissipating vital creative energies in the endless search for cash. Speaking only of the theatre panel of the National Endowment for the Arts, where I served for two years under the leadership of Ruth Mayleas, we were always struggling to reward theatres of quality in the face of pressure to distribute grants on a geographical basis. The fact that professional theatres were hardly a dominant feature of life in, say, Montana or Idaho made this kind of representative democracy an absurdity, and accounted for the competing claims on the National Endowment's funds of the University Resident Theatre Association—a nationwide consortium of university drama departments, with amateur theatre groups composed almost entirely of graduate students—which is now trying to grab a slice of the limited pie.

Still, the National Endowment for the Arts, whatever its limitations, has by far the most progressive and objective standards for determining assistance to the performing arts; it provides, with the help of expert panels, relief to all qualified institutions, including the most experimental, regardless of their size or popularity.

The private foundations, on the other hand, have not, as a whole, proved as scrupulous or faithful in their support of performing arts organizations, partly because of limitations in their staffs and partly because of an oversensitivity to fashion. Certainly these foundations have been helpful to the arts, but they lack the Endowment's evenhandedness; their reluctance to provide basic support for more than brief circumscribed periods has made their granting of awards, and their withdrawal of awards, sometimes look whimsical and capricious.

One problem is the vagueness of criteria. Either these private foundations lack confidence in their own judgments or have special interests that color their decisions. To illustrate the first instance, I am reminded of an attempt, during the First Annual Congress of Theatre (FACT) at Princeton last June, by a representative of a small Midwestern foundation to "quantify subjective criteria," as she called her effort to define the standards and procedures of her board of directors. Among the criteria weighed by this board, she said, were quality of leadership, quality of planning, quality of community impact, quality of fiscal management, quality of audience development—in short, everything but artistic quality. The standards, in other words, were not aesthetic but rather sociological, educational, and administrative, since these were more easily measured; nobody on this particular foundation, apparently, was willing to make a simple judgment on an applicant theatre's values and record.

The larger foundations, on the other hand, are even less specific about their criteria, especially since they are usually reluctant to play the role of passive benefactor willing to provide straight operating funds, and prefer rather an interventionist role that encourages institutions to innovate with what is colloquially called "funny money" (grants for special projects) and that even helps to initiate new arts institutions (as the Ford Foundation did with the short-lived Mummer's Theatre in Oklahoma). This suggests that the directors of these private foundations are sometimes under a compulsion to be "creative" themselves. And since such foundations are often more social-minded than artistically oriented, the applicant institution frequently finds itself twisted into contortions in order to find some new project that might attract financial attention: video-taped performances, school tours, children's shows, seminars with the audience, senior-citizen specials, minority-group appeals—anything, in fact, but the basic programs that make up artistic identity.

Furthermore, these larger foundations tend to favor certain kinds of enterprises over others—guided not by quality but by the special prejudices of their directors. For example, the Ford Foundation—far and away the largest benefactor of the arts (it gave $109 million between 1965 and 1971, compared with $15 million from the Rockefeller Foundation, its closest competitor)—was unquestionably largely responsible for the growth of the resident theatre movement in America, which owes its present strength to the unflagging support of W. McNeil Lowry, the foundation's former director of arts and humanities. But because of Mr. Lowry's strong personal conviction that the professional arts could never flourish in a university setting, no professional university-based arts institution, to my knowledge, has ever received support from the Ford Foundation; it was only because of the backing of the Rockefeller Foundation, which—under *its* arts and humanities director, Norman Lloyd—took the opposite view, that Mr. Lowry's opinion did not become a self-fulfilling prophecy.

Other lacunae are even more curious. While the Ford Foundation made grants amounting to $29.7 million to Lincoln Center in New York City, $5 million to the Kennedy Center in Washington, D.C., $5 million to the American Conservatory Theatre in San Francisco, $3.5 million to the Alley Theatre in Houston, and almost $2 million to the Mummer's Theatre, among many others, it never recognized the existence of one of the most enterprising institutions in the country, the New York Shakespeare Festival. As Stuart W. Little describes it, in his recent biography of Joseph Papp: "Throughout the history of the Festival, in the face of repeated requests and even pleas for help, during a period when rather large grants were being made to almost every other theatre organization in the country, Ford gave not one penny to Papp, and the fat file folders of correspondence stored just outside Papp's office, covering 15 years of request and rejection, revealed exchanges that were acrimonious and bitter." (Some of these exchanges are preserved in the book, and they make fascinating reading.)

In the early days, the Ford Foundation used to argue that free Shakespeare in Central Park was unfair competition for Broadway; later, it was more vague as to its reasons for ignoring Papp. Lowry merely expressed "difficulty" in seeing how the Public Theatre season would fit into Ford's program for the theatre, which included "production opportunities for the new playwrights." (Papp's season included the Pulitzer Prize-winning *No Place to Be Somebody.*) In the face of such a reply, it was understandable that Papp would complain in a letter to Lowry's superior, McGeorge Bundy, that "it was certainly humiliating to go around hat in hand after achieving national and international prominence as a theatre institution and being subjected to quaint and ill-informed opinions about standards in the arts." (Bundy's reply was equally curt.) Interestingly enough, it was not until Papp joined the establishment network by taking over Lincoln Center that the Ford Foundation swallowed whatever bitterness it felt toward him and made the Beaumont a grant of $1.5 million, spread out over three years.

This controversy suggests some of the problems regarding private foundations and the arts: lacking a sufficiently large permanent staff or sufficient consultants, these foundations are inclined to become too dependent on the whims and prejudices of their directors, if indeed the directors are not being overruled by board members even more ignorant of the special needs of artists. It is remarkable, considering the large amounts of tax-free funds dispensed annually by these foundations, that they make so little effort at public accountability; now that some of them are preparing to cut their arts budgets even further, the likelihood is that their choices will grow even more conservative, if not subject entirely to arbitrary internal decisions.

So what of the future of the performing arts in America? It looks dismal. At a time when more and more people are discovering the pleasures of culture, the financial base for these arts is gradually crumbling. The National Endowment is growing too slowly; the private foundations are retrenching; the business community is still largely self-interested; and the "private sector" is being staggered by the growing inflation. One can foresee the day, if some radical solution isn't discovered quickly, when many of these performing arts organizations will be closing their doors.

There is one way, however, in which the "private sector" can still have some impact on the performing arts—not by financial contribution, which will always be minimal (and negligible for experimental groups), but rather by social and political pressure in demanding that the formal agencies take on more responsibility. The government must be made to realize that the arts have a value to the nation at least one-hundredth that of defense—to acknowledge this would solve the problem immediately—or, alternatively, the government must be induced to assume its proper obligations in regard to health, poverty, science, education, and urban problems, so that private foundations, which now contribute 86 percent of their annual budgets to these programs, could increase rather than shrink their already meager 9 percent share to the arts and humanities. But this solution requires not only a compassionate administration but an enlightened citizenry, one that recognizes the importance of the arts to the spiritual well-being of the nation. For the soul, as a Bernard Shaw character has observed, is a very expensive thing to keep: "It eats music and pictures and books and mountains and lakes and beautiful things to wear and nice people to be with. In this country you can't have them without lots of money; that is why our souls are so horribly starved." Only when this kind of food is recognized, in our own starved country, as essential nourishment for intellectual, emotional, and spiritual growth—and not just a luxury in affluent times—will the crisis threatening the performing arts come to an end.   (1974)

Theatre and the University

Whenever I hear of another performing arts center being dedicated at some college or university, I think of a scene in Luis Buñuel's early surrealist film, *L'Age d'Or,* where dwarf officials in frock coats, mumbling banalities against a desolate background of sea and sky, deposit a load of horse manure on a cornerstone. Buildings of this kind have been proliferating on the campus in recent years, and the desire to apostrophize these inanimate structures of bricks and mortar, glass, wood, and cement proceeds less, I think, from a love of art or architecture than a fear of mutability—a need to transcend the impermanence of flesh and blood, an Ozymandias-like compulsion to display proud works to the mighty and make them despair.

I mean no disrespect for the architects who design such structures, or the artisans who plan and execute them, when I urge that we concentrate our limited reserves of celebration on what is living, human, and in motion—particularly when a building is devoted to performance. Put another way, the test of any new theatre structure will ultimately be the kind of work to be found inside it in the future. I have seen too many university performance centers standing empty and purposeless on the campus not to know that the time to celebrate a building is more properly at the end, rather than at the beginning, of its life, since only then will its human function have become manifest and clear.

It may be that I speak out of a hidden envy, because the performing arts in my own bailiwick at Yale are relatively ill-housed, being relegated to an outdated Broadway-type proscenium stage (where student acting projects take place) and a converted, deconsecrated Baptist church (where our resident professional company performs, supported by a few resident bats). Still, I have learned over the years that the quality of a theatre building is considerably less important than the quality of the spirit that inhabits it, and not all the technological advances in the world—not electronic switchboards or computerized light plots or elevated platforms or revolving stages or convertible black boxes—can create a work of art when that spirit is missing. (It's hard enough to create effective theatre when the spirit is willing.)

It seems to me less appropriate, therefore, to dedicate a work of theatre architecture on a university campus than to invoke the spirit that should preside over it. And the spirit I have in mind is one that has been a little in disgrace in recent years, though it just may be coming back in favor—the elusive, indefinable spirit of excellence.

By the spirit of excellence, I mean not just professionalism, though that is implied in the phrase, but rather a certain fanatical and ruthless refusal to settle for half in any creative endeavor. The performance facilities of higher education can be very effectively employed by students for self-expression in the arts—I see real value in that use—but it is my belief that under the proper conditions the university is capable of much more: it can provide the base for genuine artistic renewal in all areas of performance—theatre, music, and dance.

This idea, which was first advanced by Eric Bentley in 1946 in his book *The Playwright as Thinker*, may appear debatable today, but twenty-eight years ago it must have seemed totally implausible. Indeed, as recently as 1961, in a speech delivered to a group of graduate deans, W. McNeil Lowry—then director of the Ford Foundation's program in arts and humanities—pronounced what sounded like a death sentence on the relationship between the university and the creative arts. In that address, he affirmed that while colleges and universities had the facilities and the money and the talent for training and performance in the arts, they did not provide the proper atmosphere, largely because it was in our institutions of higher learning that amateurism and dilettantism were firmly installed and exalted. He reached three conclusions: (1) "The university has largely taken over the functions of professional training in the arts but, in the main, has sacrificed professional standards in doing so. . . . (2) The trend is irreversible. . . .

(3) The requisite shift in the university environment for the arts will be achieved only under great difficulties, if at all. . . ."

Thirteen years later, at a time when many universities have the talent, some have the facilities, and virtually none have the money, it is possible to examine Mr. Lowry's conclusions to see whether they were prophetic. And it must be conceded at the outset that, for the most part, his diagnosis was correct and his prognosis realistic. The problem is not so much that our institutions of higher learning have encouraged dabbling in the arts—part-time painting, dramatic-society acting, or weekend orchestra. Such activities, as I hope to show later, are not only an important adjunct of liberal education, but also a necessary prelude to serious practice and appreciation. The problem, rather, is that the university has embraced amateur *standards* as a measure of creative achievement and, in so doing, has reduced the distance between attempt and accomplishment, between neophyte effort and artistic achievement.

To be fair about it, the university was under tremendous pressure from its constituency, especially during the sixties, to suppress any values that might smack of "elitism," including the notion that the educational process existed partly for the development of taste or intelligence. During this period of student unrest, professional excellence was identified by many as a source of oppression, while a craze for "participation" resulted in the momentary eclipse of the talented and the trained. Education was leveled; the university was evaluated according to its service to the community; the arts were being subjected to the litmus test of social utility. Once again, cultural skills were identified with political inequality; once again, one heard the voice of Dostoevsky's revolutionary theorist Shigalov, in *The Possessed*, announcing that since men of talent tend to rise, Cicero's tongue must be torn out, Copernicus's eyes gouged out, and Shakespeare stoned.

It was not simply that a few feverish, thoughtless students were using their hatred of inequality as an occasion for disrupting any performance that did not overtly further their cause; it was, rather, that the university itself, traditionally the

home for the best that had been thought and created, had begun to lose its nerve in regard to its own purpose, and to question the importance of literature, theatre, art, and music. Only
later would people begin to realize that the revolutionary
values of radical students regarding art and the humanities
were very similar to the philistine values of commercial
society; and that the levelers on the left and the right had
joined hands against the university and the creative arts in a
common effort to obliterate all undemocratic (unprofitable?)
standards and distinctions.

Does this mean, as Mr. Lowry concluded, that colleges and
universities are forever doomed to inspire amateurism, destined to discourage those with a serious interest in the arts?
Can these institutions simultaneously sustain the creative spirit
and maintain their status as centers of liberal learning? Will a
decent respect for artistic standards be preserved in the university without the presence of more professional performers,
more rigorous admission procedures, and more practical emphasis in all the arts areas?

At this particular time, during a rising inflation and growing
unemployment, when most universities are too poor to support
their basic programs, much less the added burdens of expensive
resident performance groups, and when even the Ford Foundation is considering a 50 percent cut in its grant allocations,
there would seem to be no positive answer to these questions.
Still, a positive answer must be found if the arts are going
to have any future in this country. For I persist in my peculiar
but passionate conviction that the university remains the
brightest hope not just for the preservation but also for the
development of high culture in America. I say this less on the
evidence of what the university has achieved thus far—though
it can boast of real success in recent years—than on the fact
that it enjoys a special position as the locus of youth and age,
experiment and tradition, art and intellect, working process
and realized results, apprenticeship and professionalism, the
possibilities of the future and the heritage of the past. And I
say this most of all because, regardless of the derelictions and
failures of the sixties, I believe the university can still regain

its position as a center of standards in a society that tends
to base its artistic values on what is fashionable, newsworthy,
novel, and chic.

This is not to suggest that undergraduate colleges should
professionalize their arts programs, and begin recruiting resident theatre companies, dance companies, and chamber
quartets. Quite the contrary. My own sense is that the undergraduate college can continue to serve, as it has been serving,
as a breeding ground for future artists and audiences through
courses in theory and practice, through extracurricular student
performances, and through occasional recitals by visiting artists
or professional faculty as goal-models. No, it is the graduate
schools of the arts, rather, that should be transformed into
professional conservatories, throwing overboard such useless
academic ballast as degree requirements, sabbatical leaves,
short course loads, tenure, and the like, recruiting faculty from
among working professionals in the field, seeking out talent
rather than grades in their entering students, and—this is very
necessary—developing a professional resident company with
which advanced conservatory students can apprentice and into
which they can graduate, if they are qualified.

What I am suggesting is that the undergraduate college provide the soil and climate for the seed that the professional
school will later transplant and cultivate. Colleges are
equipped neither by inclination nor charter to be professional
conservatories or vocational schools, nor should they attempt
a halfhearted training in order to please their artistically
inclined students. But they *can* provide a valuable preprofes-
sional service by arousing curiosity in a student's mind, an
appetite for the arts, and, most difficult and necessary of all,
a respect for excellence and a sense of humility. In this
manner, colleges can function—as they are forced to function
in America at the present time—as a substitute for the culture
that Europeans absorb quite naturally from their home and
their society.

For it is an unhappy fact of our own society that it is
virtually barren of the cultural qualities that other peoples
draw from the air, and that is why our institutions of higher
learning are bearing such a heavy responsibility for cultural

development. In England, for example, a young person makes immediate contact with the best drama, music, and literature available simply by turning his television dial to the BBC, or by picking up a ticket to the provincial rep or the local symphony, which may explain why a young man or woman can begin acting training as early as sixteen in any of the English drama schools without fear of being unfamiliar with the texts to be performed, or ignorant of the background that might make the performance more texturized and rich.

In our country, on the other hand, the TV channels are more likely to be dominated by *The Waltons* and *Planet of the Apes* than by *War and Peace* and *Uncle Vanya*, while the local theatre is usually a dinner theatre, serving up *Hello, Dolly* and *The Sunshine Boys*. (Even our more serious cultural institutions often seem off limits to the young, being populated largely with the middle-aged and the middle class.) That is why colleges have a potential for service beyond the declarations in their catalogues: without changing their function, they are capable of instilling a sense of literature, a love of music, a feeling for art, and a response to theatre in their students—often for the very first time. The extent of actual practice in the arts, under such circumstances, is a variable determined by both the student's desire and the institution's facilities; but however extensive the craft courses, they should never confuse the student about his or her own capacities in relation to professional standards—which are fixed by the finest work currently being done in the field.

If, as a result of this college study and practice, the student decides to train seriously in any of the professional arts, then application should be encouraged, following completion of the undergraduate curriculum, to one of the several conservatories of training. And it is in those conservatories that the total devotion required of the artist will be cultivated, along with strict attention to the skills, techniques, goals, and ideals of the art form. I do not believe, however, that any of these things can be effectively learned in a conservatory without the presence there of gifted professional artists as teachers and role-models, and preferably also as the nucleus of a resident performance company, for the practice—so prevalent among members of the so-called University Resident Theatre Association—of creating graduate student companies, even when salted with one or two professional actors or directors, is a virtual guarantee that the standards of performance will be lowered, in the minds of both students and audiences.

Admittedly, the development of a professional resident company in the university is fraught with difficulty, given the economy, the limitations on facilities, the envy of students in training, and the time it takes to achieve ensemble cohesion. But I believe it to be an essential of any training process in America, regardless of the difficulties, and its effectiveness can be quickly measured by the quality of the students who have benefited from it. As for those who say that such professionalism has no place on the campus, they should reflect on the analogy of the medical school, which uses the professional facilities of the hospital in the same manner for training its students, or of the science laboratory, where the professional researcher and his advanced students collaborate in developing new techniques of experimentation and discovery.

In short, if the college provides the hothouse environment for curiosity about the creative arts, and the professional school provides the training in those arts when students grow serious enough to pursue the profession intently, then the professional nucleus puts the training to practical use, either as a place for early apprenticeship and later employment or as a model that regulates and determines the thrust of the training. In this manner, the university can support that vertical structure that brings the student from embryonic interest to mature achievement without violating the precepts of liberal education or professional training.

But, it may be asked, how can we guarantee that the professional nucleus will effectively inform the goals and values of the training, considering the difficulties I have mentioned? There is no guarantee; there is only the hope that, whatever the external pressures, such a nucleus will maintain its stability—and only the faith that, whatever the internal shortcomings, it will continue to be propelled forward by a tireless pursuit of art. For I have left unmentioned one element in our vertical combination beyond the people and the institutions without which the very notion of standards is a hollow concept—and that is the Platonic idea of art itself, the shadow on the walls of the cave that signals us obscurely how far we still must go. Which brings me back to the spirit I invoked at the beginning—a spirit that, however enfeebled in recent years, has managed to stay alive in a culture primarily characterized by complacency, sloth, mediocrity, security, timidity, and received ideas. And thank God it has, for without it we are not alive. As the poet William Blake wrote, during another bad time:

> Degrade first the arts if you'd mankind degrade.
> Hire idiots to paint with cold light and hot shade;
> Give high price for the worst, leave the best in disgrace,
> And with labours of ignorance fill every place.

Lest we fill the few best places that remain with labors of ignorance, these words should be written in fire on the walls of every performance center in the land. (1974)

News Theatre

A powerful phenomenon has begun to shape the cultural and political events of our time. Let us, for want of a better term, call it "news theatre." By news theatre, I don't mean documentary plays or theatre of fact or living newspapers, but a histrionic proceeding that results from a collaboration between newsworthy personalities, a vast public, and the visual or print media (television, films, book publishing, magazines, and newspapers).

News theatre, in other words, is any event that confuses news with theatre and theatre with news. When Norman Mailer sells tickets to a crowd of prominent people for his fiftieth birthday party, promising an announcement of world importance, and then tells the assembled guests that he is forming a counterintelligence agency to keep tabs on the FBI and the CIA, *that* is news theatre, because it represents the mutual exploitation of the media by Mailer and Mailer by the media for theatrical purposes.

It is news theatre when a California family agrees to expose before television cameras the most intimate secrets of its family life, including marital strife and divorce and the homosexual inclinations of one of the children. It is news theatre when the Symbionese Liberation Army kidnaps the daughter of a newspaper magnate and then designs its every move to capture and dominate the media, whether through publicity for a food distribution program, or its demand to have two imprisoned members appear on television, or its choice of a bank with automatic cameras so that a robbery can be photographically recorded. (The apocalyptic demise of six members of the SLA in a flaming Los Angeles house, as seen on television, is also a form of news theatre.)

It is news theatre when Arab guerrillas are able to command the attention of the world's media by assassinating eleven members of the Israeli Olympic team or by blowing up a hijacked airliner or by gunning down innocent children in a Ma'alot schoolhouse. And it is news theatre when President Nixon takes on the road a show called Operation Candor (being a turkey, it closed out of town some months ago), laboring to convince American audiences of his "credibility" after the Watergate disclosures, despite the tremor in his hands and the moisture drenching his upper lip. Indeed, the very idea of "credibility" may be only another convention of news theatre. It is certainly more appropriate to the art of acting than to the craft of government, since it has less to do with verifying facts or discovering truth than with simulating a role of sincerity before the people.

Obviously, in describing the phenomenon of news theatre, I am not announcing anything original or startling. I suspect Daniel Boorstin was talking about the same thing in his book *The Image*, when he formulated his concept of the "pseudo-event." On the other hand, I hope I may be able to examine the idea from a somewhat different perspective, given my theatrical background, and given what is proving to be a somewhat obsessive interest in the moral price exacted by fame in this country. Nor can I pretend to speak as a detached observer: I am myself a participant in news theatre, and possibly another one of its victims. Anybody engaged in public activities tends to become an actor of a sort; merely to speak before an audience is to become something of a histrionic figure, self-consciously involved with posture, gesture, delivery.

Beyond this, however, public figures in our time tend to be pressured by their very notoriety into becoming actors. It is only one step from the television newsroom, for example— where commentators are usually chosen more on the basis of such theatrical qualities as their looks and voices than on their capacity to analyze the news—to the movies or the stage. Consider the career of Jim Bouton, who went from the playing fields to the newsroom of CBS to a featured role in Robert Altman's movie *The Long Goodbye.* Or consider Howard Cosell, sports announcer for ABC, who appeared in Woody Allen's *Bananas,* and is now preparing to run for political office. (Former Cleveland Mayor Carl Stokes took the opposite route, going from politics to the newsroom of NBC.)

Consider, too, the CBS theatre reviewer Leonard Harris, who recently played the reporter in *Born Yesterday* at the Manhattan Theatre Club. Or consider more personal examples, in the prospect of two heads of Eastern drama schools appearing as actors on the public stage: John Houseman of Juilliard has won a well-deserved Academy Award for his role in *The Paper Chase,* and I myself completed a run some months ago, playing President Nixon in the Yale Repertory Theatre production of *Watergate Classics.*

I trust that all of us will be forgiven for extending our functions into theatrical performance; such lapses from official duties are harmless, and also rather relaxing. I mention them only to lend weight to my point that once you have become a public man in media America you have, willy-nilly, joined that great coast-to-coast repertory company that constitutes the only national theatre we have. As Jimmy Durante used to complain, everybody's getting into the act; but oddly enough it's only in recent years that cultural personalities have assumed enough interest for the world at large to qualify as actors in news theatre.

If I am worried by the more extreme manifestations of this development, it is because of its potentially malign effect on the moral direction of an artist's life, to say nothing of the corruption of his privacy. It is certain that the media now possess the power to create, perpetuate, and destroy the reputations of gifted people in this country through excessive exposure or excessive neglect, for although an individual may qualify as an actor in news theatre through some genuine personal achievement, the length of his run is determined exclusively by the media, either with or without the connivance of the public.

Before I say why I find this lamentable, however, it might be wise to talk a little about the origins of the form and about some of its ramifications, and to reflect, too, on why this age has become so histrionic. Apparently in response to an insatiable public hunger for human symbols and icons, we tend to personify everything in America these days, from commercial products such as Cap'n Crunch cereal and Jolly Green Giant peas to political parties, cultural institutions, and collaborative works of art. We attempt to put human faces even on faceless entities, perhaps out of nostalgia for mythical figures who might replace our lost gods and ceremonial persons. And just as primitive people endowed their leaders and shamans with curative powers, and subjects of royalty were convinced their kings had the power to cure through touch, so Americans still long to believe, in an age without magic, that certain specially endowed individuals can heal our disorders, realize our dreams, and solve our problems through the intervention of their powerful, magnetic personalities.

In a democratic society, this means that all Americans have potentially available to them the kind of fame previously reserved only for royalty—or, to speak in terms of our own royalty, the kind of notoriety once enjoyed only by movie stars. This unprecedented opportunity for celebrity inevitably creates an unprecedented *desire* for celebrity—especially now that social mobility has become relatively restricted through its traditional avenues of business and politics, and therefore open primarily through avenues of culture or publicity.

As a result of this development, the quest for fame has recently begun to outstrip the desire for money or power as the central animating motive of American life; and fame, we should note, has the most theatrical consequences of the three. One can be wealthy and obscure; one can even be powerful and still play a backstage role; but to be famous is, by definition, to be a role-playing animal, to abandon the private self for the public mask.

Add to this the overwhelming desire displayed by contemporary Americans to establish a sense of personal identity in a mass society. The need to escape obscurity, to validate existence, is becoming almost a national obsession in our crowded time, leading to gratuitous acts that seem to have no greater purpose than to attract the attention of the media. A relatively harmless example of this is the impulse to scrawl graffiti over the walls of New York subways, most of them signed with a code name, in a bid for simultaneous credit and anonymity.

A more sinister instance is the kind of violent public act increasingly being committed in America for the sake of achieving immediate celebrity. The frequency of assassination attempts in America since the invention of television must surely have theatrical as well as ideological causes. Think of Arthur Bremer's smiling face after his attempt on the life of George Wallace, delighted at having caught the attention of the camera, a more sinister version of all those ordinary people who wave frantically at the TV cameras as they pan past their faces in a street or a studio.

What I am trying to suggest is that news theatre threatens to make of all the world a stage, and players out of all the men and women. In so doing, it removes our attention from the deed to the actor of the deed, making us concentrate on a personality or a temperament rather than an issue or an action. Of course, the actor would not have much significance were it not for some significant initial action, but after the attention-getting moment is past, the rest is usually pure theatre. Now, in saying this, I do not wish to denigrate the importance of theatre, or its value as entertainment; I could hardly do this, given my own function as one who helps to create theatre, as one who occasionally criticizes it, and as one who usually enjoys watching it. No, my concern is rather for the unfortunate actor, since he almost invariably loses the meaning of his original unrehearsed act in a performance that often lacks sincerity and, worse, that sometimes casts unnecessary doubts upon the validity of his original deed.

Take, as an example, the case of Daniel Berrigan, who first came to public notice after a heroic act of resistance to the Vietnam war—the burning of draft records at Catonsville, for which he was later imprisoned in Danbury jail. Berrigan's difficult action, committed in public along with eight other war resisters, did much to dramatize the lengths to which people of conscience were willing to go in order to express their moral objections to the war. But it was not long before this priest and poet—the passionate, altruistic man who burned the draft records—was being swallowed up inside a self-conscious, self-exonerating, slightly self-intoxicated actor, encouraged by the media to pronounce upon a variety of political subjects in a rhetoric swollen with accents of divine inspiration.

Furthermore, Berrigan soon felt impelled to transfer his theatrical impulses to the actual stage in the form of a quasi-documentary, considerably overpraised at the time, called *The Trial of the Catonsville Nine*. Here he tried to justify his initial act of civil disobedience not only as a moral necessity but as a legal principle, satirizing the presiding judge who had evaluated the case according to judicial rules as some kind of flaccid liberal ninny who lacked the courage to acquit everybody purely on the basis of their moral beauty. In taking this tack, Father Berrigan actually managed to drain some of the real beauty from his act, since civil disobedience tends to lose its stature when promulgated as an action without a consequence.

I couldn't help thinking, at the time, of another work about the difficulty of discriminating between the dictates of morality and the law—Herman Melville's *Billy Budd*—in which a similar judge, required to adjudicate a crime committed out of virtuous motives, was nevertheless forced to convict a man he recognized as a saint in order to preserve the painful imperatives of the legal system. Instead of being scorned, this judge was blessed by his victim at the moment of his execution—blessed because Billy Budd understood the conflict between the laws of God and the laws of man, and sensed the anguish Captain Vere was suffering in trying to reconcile them. But this, I think, suggests the difference between true saints and those created by news theatre, just as it demonstrates the difference between complex works of art formulated by real artists and acts of self-justification engineered by one of the interested parties.

I hope it is clear that I have great respect for the original sacrifice of Father Berrigan. If I emphasize the histrionic aspect of Berrigan's later development, it is in order to illustrate how, by theatricalizing such things, news theatre helps to rob them of their significance, to lower their value through its stimulation of the theatrical. A vivid demonstration of this could be seen in the closing moments of Berrigan's play, which consisted of a three-minute film clip taken at the actual burning of the records and the arrest of the people involved. The resisters stand solemnly and ceremoniously around the fire; the police vans arrive to take them off to the station house. Berrigan walks briskly to the van accompanied by a police officer and, just before he steps in, turns fully around to look for the camera. This very human moment of vanity, captured on film, was perhaps more telling in its way than all the posturing, declamation, and rhetoric of the play.

In the political sphere, one could name many more examples of good people contorted into artificial attitudes by the presence and pressure of the media: Daniel Ellsberg, who has seemed, after his decision to publish the Pentagon Papers, to be conducting one long, continuous interview, fixed in a heroic frieze that includes the perpetually upturned smile of his admiring wife; Sam Ervin, brought to worldwide attention through his role in the Watergate hearings, now cast eternally as a homiletic rustic philosopher, complete with bouncing eyebrows, gnarled hands, and best-selling records and books of proverbialisms; Martha Mitchell, converting what might be genuine pain and embarrassment over the precipitous turn in her family fortunes into a mode of performance through well-planned telephone calls and television appearances.

Even foreign figures often find themselves entrapped inside the network of American news theatre. Think of Aleksandr Solzhenitsyn, the very embodiment in Western eyes of resistance against censorship and oppression until the moment when, exiled from the Soviet Union, he overexposed himself in public with a series of questionable pronunciamentos and then disappeared behind a virtual curtain of media silence, to the dismay of all those who had been depending on him to publicize their plight. One hardly knows whom to blame in cases like this—the media, whose fickleness concerning personalities keeps them prominent only as long as they are newsworthy, or the personalities themselves, provoked by the fear of losing attention into ever bolder and more theatrical actions.

Much of this is inevitable in an age when the domination of television and the newspapers has turned the world into a vast global theatre, when a huge audience of millions is continually gorging on the entertainment value of news. Those who have had an opportunity to watch Jack Ruby kill Lee Harvey Oswald on camera, or Mark Essex shooting down policemen and passers-by from the roof of a New Orleans Howard Johnson's before being gunned down himself, have been conditioned to expect moments of high drama with which to fill their leisure hours. (Isn't the relatively harmless fashion of "streaking" an effort to introduce media sensationalism into the routine of everyday events?)

Somebody has to appear on the covers of *Time* and *Newsweek* every seven days, somebody has to be interviewed by Johnny Carson, or Merv Griffin, or Dick Cavett, or David Susskind; somebody has to be worthy of interest on the *Today*, the *Tonight*, and the *Tomorrow* shows. When a candidate for President of the United States consents to appear on *Laugh-In*, then we know that politicians have recognized the primal value of the entertainment industry, and there is little left to distinguish government from show business or current events from coming attractions.

Even a vicious and violent war can become a form of pre-

and post-prandial entertainment, as we learned during the period of Vietnam, in which viewing the death and mutilation of soldiers and the suffering of napalmed civilians could suffice to carry us through the cocktail hour and the period before bedtime.

As Daniel Boorstin has observed, "We need not be theologians to see that we have shifted responsibility for making the world interesting from God to the newspaperman." And we all contribute to this clamor for excitement—even those who, like myself, express their opposition to it—for news theatre is so compelling that it is virtually impossible, short of banning all organs of communication from the house, to turn one's eyes from its hypnotic fascinations. For this reason, I must try to do what for me is a difficult thing—namely, to avoid the delicious temptations of outrage and indignation—and instead attempt to explain, as coolly as possible, why I have come to believe that news theatre is having such a pernicious effect on the quality of our arts and the state of our culture. (Its corruption of our politics has already been accomplished.)

It seems clear that the very thing that poets and intellectuals have desired for years has now come to pass—they have begun to achieve almost as much prominence as movie stars and politicians. From the day in 1965 that Robert Lowell refused to appear at President Johnson's White House Festival of the Arts, and the *Times* printed the story on the front page, it was obvious that cultural figures had begun to emerge into the political limelight in America, until now hardly anybody is surprised to find a number of artists and intellectuals on the American equivalent of the Queen's List in England—the enemies list of Richard Nixon.

Clearly, the public that was previously interested only in politicians, businessmen, revolutionaries, protesters, gangsters, theatre celebrities, and Presidential cronies has now begun to turn its eyes toward writers, thinkers, composers, painters, poets, journalists, and critics. But instead of bringing about that Platonic Republic in which kings would be turned into philosophers, this development threatens to change the philosophers into politicians. To transform creative individuals into figures of the news, to convert complex questions of art into a species of personality exploitation, is, I think, to narrow the possibilities of growth, development, and renewal in the very places where they are most desperately needed.

One of my texts for this theme is the career of Norman Mailer, a figure about whom I have grown increasingly apprehensive over the past years—not because I lack respect for his talent, but rather because this talent has proved so vulnerable to external pressures. Mailer personifies most dramatically the kind of havoc that news theatre can visit on a creative personality. I have written elsewhere, perhaps too insistently, regarding my concern over Mailer's journey from a fiction writer, to a writer of confessional autobiography, to a candidate for political office, to a journalist for *Life* and *Esquire,* and finally to director and star of his own home movies. To some, this has looked like the career of a modern Renaissance man, a Leonardo of the present age, and there is no question that his reach has been ambitious. My question is about the scope of his actual accomplishment. Mailer has always seemed to me less interested in sublimating his gifts through art or invention than in aggrandizing his personality through publicity. In short, too much of his energy has been wasted in self-promotion and public relations through the encouragement of both the consumers and the producers of news theatre.

Harvey Swados observed some years ago that the publishing industry was dominated by three names—Ernest Hemingway, Norman Mailer, and J. D. Salinger—all of whom had managed to prosper as authors partly because they could be exalted as "personalities." But of the three, only Mailer has consciously pursued this crown. Hemingway, we should remember, remained an expatriate from America most of his creative life, while Salinger made a deliberate decision for exile from the media, living in total isolation from reporters and interviewers in northern New England. In brief, only Mailer can be said to have thrown himself into the circus of news theatre and tried to manipulate the cultural scene for his own advantage.

Unlike the others, Mailer elected to acknowledge the show-business side of himself, motivated partly by ambition, partly by ego, partly by experiment, as if he could simultaneously profit by the culture's appetite for personalities and exploit it for creative purposes, through an act of personal transcendence. Almost ten years ago, Norman Podhoretz (then one of Mailer's strongest supporters) observed this effort with considerable approval, hailing Mailer's career as "exemplary" because it was devoted to what Podhoretz claimed to be the primary question of American life: "Whether the pursuit of success need cripple a man spiritually, whether a man can work through the corruptions inherent in that pursuit without falling into the equally disabling corruptions inherent in the stance of hypocritical high-mindedness."

High-mindedness, hypocritical or otherwise, has hardly been the most conspicuous quality of the decade that culminated in Watergate; and I have no way of knowing whether Mr. Podhoretz would still subscribe to his opinion of ten years ago, whether he still believes Norman Mailer to be leading an "exemplary career." But the intervening years have shown us something about the consequences to the spirit implicit in the pursuit of success, and I think we may now be in a position to comment upon how effectively Mailer has managed to transcend the corruptions of the culture he embraced.

Am I wrong in thinking that Mailer has now become almost completely swallowed up by his self-created role, that he perfectly fulfills Daniel Boorstin's definition of the celebrity as one "who is known for his well-knownness"? I do not doubt the value of Mailer's journalistic essays on the moonshot, on the march on the Pentagon, on the Clay-Liston fight, and so on, though I confess to doubt over whether this value is lasting. What disturbs me is how Mailer's interest in himself has begun to dominate his interest in external events. His movies are completely without quality except as further episodes in his self-generated legend. And all we know about the novel he has been announcing for the past five years is that it was sold to publishers for an unprecedented advance of $1 million.

As for Mailer's recent nonbook, a windy narrative about Marilyn Monroe accompanying a collection of photographs, it is simply a bid for increased notoriety through association with the notoriety of its subject. Full of scurrilous imputations about such rivals for glory as Arthur Miller and President Kennedy, scandalous in its confusion of fame with real achievement, it is inevitably being considered for a Broadway musical, and no doubt will one day make a full circle into a Hollywood movie, possibly with Mailer playing one of the parts. Through this work, Mailer has managed to lose himself, once and for all, in news theatre—to become, in Boorstin's words, a "human pseudo-event."

To answer Norman Podhoretz's question, then, ten years after it was asked, we must conclude that the conscious pursuit of success does indeed cripple a man spiritually in this country, regardless of the degree of his self-consciousness—or, to put the problem into the language of a previous time, one can gain the whole world and still lose one's soul. Mailer has shown us that it is impossible to work through the corruptions inherent in the pursuit of success—in that sense only can we call his career exemplary. Through his exploits and self-advertisements, Mailer has been found by the talk shows, the newspapers, the literary supplements, the pop critics, the publishers, the Broadway producers, the moviemakers—in short, by news theatre—but he has been lost to literature. I leave it to you to determine whether we should exult in what has been found . . . or mourn what has been irretrievably lost.

Obviously, figures like Mailer are more accomplices of this system than victims. But there are others who seem to be caught against their wills in the web of the media.

A poignant example of the malign effects of news theatre on a gifted individual is the case of Joseph Papp, particularly in the past year, since he took over the stewardship of two theatres at Lincoln Center. On the basis of his work with the New York Shakespeare Festival, first in Central Park and then at the Public Theatre on Lafayette Street, Papp attracted such attention over the years that the media virtually canonized him as the savior of the New York stage. And, as a matter of fact, nobody had worked so hard and so thanklessly in such a good cause. Papp had fought for years, against Park Commissioners, indifferent foundations, and the resistance of Broadway, to develop a robust free Shakespeare in Central Park; and when he opened the Public Theatre, he managed to extend his facilities to a large number of young writers, directors, actors, and designers, in an atmosphere singularly free of pressure or privilege.

Papp's experiments at the Public Theatre, like those of any theatre, were of varying quality; the importance of the place was based not on the number of its hits, but rather on its freewheeling openness, set in motion by the galvanic energy of Papp himself. Had Broadway been functioning properly, Joe Papp would undoubtedly have continued developing his theatre free of constraint as an open house of young, developing talent. The trouble was that the established theatre was in a virtual collapse and theatre commentators were surveying a barren landscape, with the result that Papp was inducted, willy-nilly, into the legions of news theatre personalities.

In little more than a year, Papp was cover-storied and interviewed in every organ of the news, and because he possessed a forceful, colorful personality, the public remained fastened on his burgeoning activities. The sense of bustle that was generated on the several stages of the Public Theatre, seen against the inert background of the commercial theatre uptown, created a sense that New York was on the brink of a theatrical renaissance that would be achieved entirely by Papp and his army of young discoveries: Jeff Bleckner, John Guare, David Rabe, Jason Miller, Dennis Reardon, Robert Montgomery, A. J. Antoon, Santa Loquasto.

It was not enough to say that the young people associated with the Public Theatre were bright and gifted; they had to be installed, according to the conventions of news theatre, in an instant hall of fame, thus invested with expectations far beyond their immediate capacity to fulfill. David Rabe, for example, on the basis of two poetically conceived plays of social conscience, was being hailed in some quarters as the finest American playwright of the decade. (Papp himself, no doubt partly out of showmanship, was declaring Rabe the logical successor to Eugene O'Neill.) Similarly, Robert Montgomery's promising fantasy on Dostoevsky's *The Idiot*, called *Subject to Fits*, was bringing extravagant praise both to him and to his young director, A. J. Antoon, despite the workshop nature of the play and the relative inexperience of the playwright.

Encouraged by the enthusiastic reception of these works, Papp soon began to transfer some of his Public Theatre successes to Broadway, hoping to fill the vacuum caused by the declining activity of the establishment producers; and it was not long before he was transferring plays to television and the movies as well. Although one of his motives for extending himself into commercial enterprises was to create a better financial base for his nonprofit theatre, the work downtown occasionally took on some of the characteristics of pre-Broadway tryouts. The blunt, roughneck, sinewy style of Papp's Shakespeare in the Park at times degenerated into the musical-comedy glitter and self-conscious ethnicity of *Two Gentlemen of Verona,* though it revived occasionally in such merry conceits as A. J. Antoon's *Much Ado About Nothing,* while the experimental probings of earlier days tended to become overshadowed by a more conventional social realism that, perhaps coincidentally, was the dominant form of Broadway. Papp never lost his scrappy courage and independence, and he continued to take risks on young talents. But a new element had entered the air of his theatre—an atmosphere of pressure, tension, competitiveness, and sometimes even panic.

There were some who even detected certain changes in the nature of the man himself. The dynamic and generous Joe Papp, whose identifying characteristic is a kind of humane democratic openness, was beginning to grow interested in empire, acquiring properties, and forming conglomerates like a nineteenth-century American tycoon. His impulse to proliferate encouraged him to look well beyond the horizons of his existing holdings, as he began assembling real estate and theatres in the same spirit that he collected talents and projects. When the Lincoln Center management was inevitably offered to Papp, it was perhaps inevitable that he would accept it, in magnificent hubristic defiance of that cursed inheritance, which, like some merciless phantom, grips the throats of all who would embrace it.

It was possible that Papp had overextended himself, and his

ambitions were exceeding his control. Around the same time he took over Lincoln Center, Papp had been formulating plans for a "national theatre" to consist partly of government-subsidized tours of Public Theatre productions, the content "popularized," as he put it in one of his manifestoes, "so it does not become a vehicle only for college professors and small college dramatic societies." Papp's design to reach large audiences with the best dramatic productions—for example, his Shakespeare in the Park offered free to anybody willing to stand on line—was now being tailored for middle America, and he even began suggesting that whatever proved offensive or difficult to such audiences should be avoided on the tour.

I mention these national ambitions in order to suggest how easy it is for news theatre to shape an image for an individual, which he is then obliged to sustain. Certainly Papp has continued to make a lot of good theatre, but he has also been encouraged to make news as well. When invited, for example, to speak informally at Yale two years ago to a group of drama students (he had taught there very effectively in 1967), he arrived accompanied by a USIA camera crew filming a documentary about him for the State Department, and proceeded to read a prepared statement to his astonished listeners with a recording device dangling from his neck.

There is something a little melancholy about this; but much more depressing is the fate being prepared for this gifted, embattled man by the media. For, as Boorstin writes, "The passage of time, which creates and establishes the hero, destroys the celebrity. The newspapers make him, and they unmake him—not by murder but by suffocation and starvation."

Papp is too irrepressible to be destroyed by the media, but there is more than a hint of animus evident in the recent treatment of him. In the very first months of his tenure at Lincoln Center, he was savagely attacked by some members of the press for doing much the same kind of work he had just been praised for, while Rabe, Bleckner, Antoon, Montgomery, and other Papp disciples are now being dismissed by reviewers as if they had never been enthroned. Some of the reviews of Rabe's *Boom Boom Room*, not to mention almost all the productions that followed at the Beaumont, the Forum, and the Public Theatre, were peculiarly contemptuous and unqualified, especially when contrasted with the hyperbolic praise lavished on Papp's productions in the past, and although Papp still has his share of defenders, I would bet that the critics and reporters are preparing to bring his celebrity to an end. Whom the media would destroy, they first make famous.

In short, Papp's days as a culture hero of news theatre are very probably numbered; and if he seems to be acting somewhat defensive and irascible these days, this may be because he senses he is an animal being prepared for sacrifice. Unquestionably, journalistic fickleness of this kind can create paranoia in the soundest man. But I see no conscious conspiracy here—merely confirmation of the fact that the only thing as newsworthy as success is failure.

The cycle being enacted here is the historical cycle of news theatre, and it is the cycle of ritual drama as well. The American celebrity—like Dionysus, Osiris, and Jesus before him—is destined to suffer rejection, if not mutilation and death. Hatred and envy are too closely linked to reverence and love. Think back to Frank Sinatra in the forties and fifties having his clothes ripped off his back by screaming admirers. Think of what would happen today to any rock singer foolish enough to enter the adoring circle of his fans.

Still, to offer anthropological explanations is hardly to condone a situation that is becoming dangerous and intolerable. By imposing the ritual of news theatre on the face of culture, the media are effectively determining that little in the way of serious culture will ever develop in New York. A process that requires calm, solitude, patience, and growth is being turned into a form of gladiatorial combat in which victims, after a moment of triumph, are mangled to bits before our eyes. Collaborative arts, involving the cooperation of many talents, are treated as if they were the creation of a single glorified individual. Poor erring mortals are intoxicated by the hubris that leads to their downfall. And men of genuine promise are cut off in their prime, either by excessive praise or excessive neglect.

What to do? Well, first, I obviously see some hope in diagnosing the condition, for the values of our culture are identical with the symptoms of the disease. Second, at the risk of sounding old-fashioned, my usual failing, I propose to those Americans unfortunate enough to qualify for news theatre that they develop the will to resist it, and to those of us inclined to watch it that we try to cultivate some admiration for character rather than for personality. Character is the intrinsic nature of the self that is expressed through behavior; personality is the external image of the self manufactured through the efforts of the media.

To abandon the mutilating rituals of news theatre is to abandon celebrity, to persist with one's work regardless of all histrionic temptations, to make a conscious sacrifice of both the appeals and the degradations of the public life. It means giving up immediate gratifications for the sake of more ulti-mate and lasting goals, pricking the side of one's intent with some spur other than fame.

This is a difficult and perhaps impossible thing to ask of talented Americans, but what is the alternative? No culture, only flashes on the evening news; no accomplishments that cannot be degraded by publicity; no truth that is not swal-lowed up in images; no heroes, only celebrities whirling dizzily in the carousel of fashion until their faces vanish in a blur. (1974)

Appendix

To the Editor of the *New York Times:*
It must take some very fancy mind juggling to write a 5,500-word essay assaulting a number of "notables" for giving themselves to the newsmedia as "willing" or "unwilling" victims, and then to submit this essay to the *New York Times* Magazine with an estimated readership of some four million people (not to mention getting paid for the job).

One would imagine that Robert Brustein's article ("News Theatre," June 16), bristling with righteous indignation and reeking with integrity, might have reasonably been submitted to *yale/theatre* magazine or at least the *New York Review of Books.* This might have been done with a quiet conscience. But no, Professor Brustein clearly chooses the most widely distributed journal in the country for his sponsor and by so doing casts himself in the very role that he seems to deplore—a willing victim of the media.

This being the case, it would have been proper to have had the author of "News Theatre" prominently displayed in the photograph illustrating his article alongside the rest of the gang of "celebrities" he attempts to dissect.

With Brustein in his proper role, some totally unknown journalist might attempt an objective job on Dean Brustein, which might go as follows:

Professor Brustein experiences the acute frustration of being so close (New Haven) yet so far from the hub of theatrical life, New York City. He wants in, but he cannot forgo the subsidized real estate offered by an Ivy League college—buildings and facilities inherited, not fought for, earned, or won. Remote from the cloisters is the New York theatre scene—cruel, abrasive, deadly competitive—where a Ph.D.

doesn't get you through the turnstile of the IRT. So he reigns under the Yale banner with Yale subsidy, one foot in New Haven and a big toe in the Big Apple.

Brustein knows as well as anyone in the theatre world that publicity (I'll use that crass word!) is the way people get to know not only what you're doing but what you're thinking. It all doesn't come out perfect, but it comes out. Without media recognition, Brustein couldn't raise a cent for his operation. Without good reviews in the *New York Times,* the Yale Drama School would be like any other drama school, which means fewer and less talented students.

Brustein's article implies that being "newsworthy" is automatically corrupt or corruptible. We all know that ivory-tower life is not ivory-pure. Corruption does not require mighty issues to test a man. It can out over a breakfast table or at lunch at Sardi's as well as at a faculty meeting. It's not where you are that breeds character, but who you are.

As for my relationships with the media, despite great shortcomings, they have been one of the single constructive forces in the development of the New York Shakespeare Festival. They have provided me with outlets for my views from the very beginning. But the right to recognition in the press and other media had to be won, in the same way the right to demand government funds to support our work had to be won. As for my being a victim of the media, a lamb being led to the slaughter, that is arrant nonsense. There is a price one must pay for success in any field—and one part of the price is becoming a target for the frustrations of others. Those who write for newspapers are no exception but perhaps more honest and kinder than those ostensible well-wishers with their self-fulfilling prophecies of my doom.

The history of my life with the New York Shakespeare Festival has been characterized by confrontations caused by a singular drive—to create a meaningful theatre for popular audiences. The attempt to thwart this drive by entrenched power or by other individuals or groups has always forced me to react in order to survive.

I never sought a confrontation with Parks Commissioner Moses. He was intent on running us out of Central Park and

I tried to prevent it. Yes, this caused a lot of front-page copy (which I did not seek) but, looking back, it proved a great service to the burgeoning New York Shakespeare Festival by bringing us to the attention of the public. It had an even more important effect by confronting the city with an important issue—that of direct municipal support for the performing arts. My battles with the Board of Estimate had nothing to do with seeking publicity. It was money we were seeking. This was what made news.

The more recent confrontation with the Columbia Broadcasting System was not of my making. What made news was not I, but CBS's cancellation of *Sticks and Bones*.

Wedding Band, the recent TV special, was banned from a number of Southern affiliate ABC stations. But I had no hand in making this news. My news was the making of the TV production, in the same way my news has been and always will be the creation of plays, television shows, or films. The artistic product is my news. The attempt to broaden the audience for new plays is my news. Finding and producing new writers is my news. Introducing and developing new directors, designers, and actors is my news. Raising funds for all of these efforts is my news.

Answering Dean Brustein's charges is *not* my news. I might have ignored the distortions of an article read by several million people, but I could not.

Joseph Papp
NEW YORK CITY

ROBERT BRUSTEIN REPLIES:

It is both sad and ironic that Joe Papp has interpreted my remarks about him in my article—an analysis of the way the media cannibalize such personalities as himself—as simply another damaging media attack, designed to bring about his downfall. In mistaking my intentions, he has triggered himself into another defensive reaction and started flailing about in all directions; but like most wild punches, his tend to land wide of the mark, when they do not contort him into contradictory stances. For example, in one paragraph he charges that

I really want to make it in New York theatre but am too frightened of the rough-and-tumble of "real life" to stray from the safe subsidies of ivied Yale; in the next, he recognizes that, like other "real-life" people "remote from the cloisters" and without Ph.D.'s, I have to raise money for our theatre, and need the media for this purpose.

I will forgo the temptation to ask Joe how, in the face of all the available evidence, he can still call New York "the hub of theatrical life," or how, in the face of my eight years in New Haven, he is able to divine that I secretly yearn to be in New York theatre. I will simply say that his final assumption is the more accurate one: like Joe, I personally am obliged to raise the entire budget for the Yale Repertory Theatre (a professional company to be distinguished from its conservatory arm of training, the Yale School of Drama) from outside private and foundation sources, and, like Joe, I find I cannot do this very effectively without some visibility for the theatre through the media.

But I conceded in the course of my article that I might very well be another victim of what I was describing, just like everyone else in a visible public position. My concern was not with striking righteous personal postures but rather with trying to diagnose the condition, examining its more extreme manifestations, and sending out a signal of distress to all those in the process of being victimized. The warning I raised had to do with a question of degree, and was issued on the assumption that although we all fall short of the ideal, this doesn't mean we should forget the ideal still exists. The important questions, I think, are these: at what point does the publicity generated by an institution for the sake of its survival fade off into the glorification of any individual identified with that institution? Is it necessary, in order to preserve and extend the life of a theatre, to change the quality and direction of its work, and, if so, it is worth it? Isn't there a line beyond which it is profitless, if not counterproductive, to venture in one's dealings with the media?

These are real questions, which I would be happy to debate with Joe in an appropriate forum, and he may have a point when he suggests that such a forum may not be the pages of a newspaper. In defense of my decision to publish the original article in the *Times,* I would say that while it is false to call its Magazine section "the most widely distributed journal in the country," it is certainly the most widely respected of the widely distributed journals, and it was essential to the aims of this particular article that it reach as many reflective people as possible. In other words, it is debatable whether the Magazine section of the *Times* is a medium of the news or an organ of ideas. What seems to be beyond debate is that the Letters column of this section, when used in an acrimonious way to reduce a discussion of ideas to a matter of personalities, is clearly a stage for news theatre. In short, this exchange between us manages to dramatize what I originally tried to describe: the pernicious and self-defeating effect of news theatre on cultural figures. (1974)

To the Editor of the *New York Times:*
The subtext of Robert Brustein's stern warning in "Broadway and the Nonprofit Theatre: A Misalliance" (August 4) to the nonprofit theatre community to beware of entangling Broadway alliances is that presentation on Broadway of a play originated in a nonprofit theatre is *by definition* corrupting. Is this really true? Was the Long Wharf Theatre derailed from its artistic course by the presentation on Broadway of *The Changing Room*? Has Arena Stage sold out as a consequence of *The Great White Hope* and *Raisin*? Is Joe Papp looking only for hits after *That Championship Season* and *Two Gentlemen of Verona*? I don't think so.

It would certainly be destructive for nonprofit resident theatres to tailor their work to mass tastes, to strive to produce "commercial" plays that would succeed on Broadway, but no one is advocating this kind of theatre-making, and it is not, despite Mr. Brustein's fears, a necessary consequence of occasional Broadway transfers of nonprofit plays. Broadway has its faults, but it is not Transylvania. For decades it was the principal fountain of serious original drama in this country, and it can spout again.

It is axiomatic that theatre art should have the widest

possible audience. If *A Moon for the Misbegotten* had closed after its initial three-week engagement last summer at a summer-stock playhouse near Chicago, several hundred thousand people would have been denied a sublime theatre experience which they could have received nowhere but in New York.

The artists who direct our nonprofit theatres—the Joe Papps, Zelda Fichandlers, Gordon Davidsons, and Arvin Browns—have shown themselves to be persons of integrity and seriousness of purpose. There is more reason to believe that they will use Broadway as it should be used, as a larger and financially rewarding arena for plays of merit, than there is to think they will succumb to crass expediency.

Alexander H. Cohen
NEW YORK, N.Y.

ROBERT BRUSTEIN REPLIES:

Alexander Cohen brings up real questions, doubting whether productions on Broadway by resident theatres can have a corrupting effect on their goals and purposes. Though I share his admiration for the integrity of the directors he mentions, I fear that their theatres are already showing the consequences of this misalliance. The Long Wharf, for example, is celebrating its tenth anniversary this fall without having more than one or two of its regular company in residence in New Haven—the rest will be in New York preparing to open *The National Health.* The Arena's *Great White Hope* was admittedly the kind of project that a nonprofit theatre would normally produce; but if it weren't for the subsequent success of this play on Broadway, I seriously doubt whether the Arena would ever have considered anything as conventional as *Raisin,* a Broadway-bound musical version of *Raisin in the Sun.* About Joe Papp and the New York Shakespeare Festival, it is unfitting for me to make any prophecies, partly because he is too unpredictable to fulfill them, partly because I have already had my say in another context. I will, therefore, let his biographer, Stuart W. Little, do the talking by quoting from his new book, *Enter Joe Papp:* "A subtle change had come over the Shakespeare Festival since the shows *That Championship Season, Sticks and Bones,* and *Two Gentlemen of Verona* were moved to Broadway . . . some added tension, some slight change of focus, an exaggerated concern for the favorable press notice, a shift away from experimental work." Since these were precisely the fears I expressed in my article, I find it highly significant to see them confirmed in the pages of an otherwise flattering biography—a book, incidentally, that Alexander Cohen himself supplied free to all members of the Princeton FACT conference. Let those members take notice, and take heed, if they are truly concerned about pre-serving theatre art in America. (1974)

FINAL NOTE: 1975

Several months after my articles and the ensuing letters were published, Joe Papp announced in a press conference that he was abandoning the experimental approach with which he had been identified. Declaring his determination to build a "national theatre" at Lincoln Center, employing "international stars" in well-known classical plays, he also affirmed that in future the work at the New York Public Theatre would con-sist largely of plays by playwrights he had already produced and directors with established reputations. "We want more care and cultivation rather than innovation and getting the young started," he said.

Two months later, in still another announcement, Papp pro-claimed that off-Broadway is dead, that he was turning the Public Theatres into workshops, and that he now intended to produce his new American plays at the Booth Theatre on Broadway. "It's a marketplace," he said. "I believe in the marketplace." Whether this represents a genuine change in direction for Mr. Papp or merely a last desperate gamble to recoup his failing fortunes, it nevertheless signifies the saddest example yet of how the marketplace absorbs serious culture into its hungry bloodstream.

Index

A NOTE ON THE TYPE

The text of this book was set in Caledonia,
a Linotype face designed by W. A. Dwiggins.
It belongs to the family of printing types called
"modern face" by printers—a term used to
mark the change in style of type letters that
occurred about 1800. Caledonia borders on the
general design of a Scotch Modern, but is more
freely drawn than that letter.

Composed, printed, and bound by
The Book Press, Brattleboro, Vermont

Typography and binding design
by Gwen Townsend